John...
Thank you for your prayers and
support. I pray that this book
is a blessing to you, your relationships,
and everyone who you reach out to.

Peace...
Brandon

UNEARTHED

How Discovering the Kingdom of
God Will Transform the Church
and Change the World

Brandon Andress

authorHOUSE®

AuthorHouse™
1663 Liberty Drive
Bloomington, IN 47403
www.authorhouse.com
Phone: 1-800-839-8640

First published by AuthorHouse   10/1/2010

ISBN: 978-1-4520-7677-5 (e)
ISBN: 978-1-4520-7675-1 (sc)
ISBN: 978-1-4520-7676-8 (hc)

Library of Congress Control Number: 2010914220

Printed in the United States of America

This book is printed on acid-free paper.

This book is dedicated to Jenny, Anna, and Caroline

for without their patient and supportive love

this work would not be possible.

*I must preach the good news of the Kingdom of God
to the other towns also, because that is why I was sent.*

*And the good news of the Kingdom of God will be preached
in the whole world as a testimony to all nations,
and then the end will come.*

- Jesus Christ

CONTENTS

FOREWORD

What do you do with a burden? You can try your best to run from it, but it haunts you and chases you wherever you go. You can try to ignore it, but then it sits and weighs on you until you submit to it. You can even try to hide from it, but it will find you and force you to pay attention to it. A burden will stay with you each and every moment of the day and will follow you around haunting you, and all you can do is pray over it. So I have continued to pray.

But God only gives you as much information as you need at any one moment and only gives you as much responsibility as you have proven to be faithful with. And that always seems to make the moments drag by and the future seem so far out of reach. Those are our seemingly unredeemable and endlessly numbered days. Those are the days when you are convinced that your prayers are not being answered. But in reality you are in the middle of them being answered. It is in those moments, those unsuspecting moments that you are being taught, refined, and molded into something usable, as long as you are willing, of course. But it is always easier to see what you have learned and how you were refined when you look back in retrospect. It is just too bad that we can't see what we are learning and how we are being refined in the moment.

Those two paragraphs sum up my experiences over the last ten years as I wrestled with a burden and wondered if my prayers were ever going to be answered. And did I mention the questions that tag along? *God, is this it? Am I doing the right things? Do you want me over here or over there? Do you want me to throw in the towel or keep pressing on? Is any of this even worth it? Am I going crazy?* But how exactly is a person supposed to think, act, or behave when God puts something on his heart of which he can't let go? It isn't like they put out manuals on *How to Act When You are in the Middle of God's Will* or anything. The closest thing we get to that is the Bible, and to be honest it really doesn't give you anything more than what you already know. You read about the second-guessers, the self-doubters, the God-doubters, and the disobeyers and all you can do is scratch your head and think, and those are the great heroes of the Bible?

But it is through those broken vessels and their faithfulness that God chooses to do his redeeming, powerful, and transformative work. And I bet that every single one of them felt very ordinary, very unworthy, and extraordinarily humbled that God would choose to use them even in a small way for His larger purposes. But it is through their, and our, inadequacies that we are reminded that it is never we who do anything spectacular in the first place, only God. And to God be all praise, honor, and glory for working and moving in spite of us.

It is not lost on me that I am an inadequate man. I meet weekly with my best friends to confess my sins, my deepest, darkest sins. And they will be the first group of people to tell you that I am not special, but that they love me anyway. I have done more to hurt people and disrupt the work of the Kingdom of God in my lifetime than I have done to move it forward. I am a doubter, a cynic, and a skeptic and I confess to you that I have even been known to roll my eyes when people tell me that God spoke to them. Not that my eye-rolling wasn't justified a few times, but my cynicism and skepticism kept me from believing that God would, or could, actually speak in a way that a person today would really hear Him. But God has a way of silencing the fools, and I was about to be silenced.

I was vacationing with my family in Tampa, Florida several years ago. There is nothing I love more than sitting on a deck overlooking the ocean, drinking freshly brewed coffee, and enjoying the warm, radiant sun while losing myself in a good book. My book of choice on this particular trip was *Wild at Heart* by John Eldredge. I would soon find out that there was not any other book in the world I should have been reading at that exact moment.

Eldredge contends in *Wild at Heart* that every man has a deep, God-given passion and calling for adventure, risk, and the pursuit of life to the fullest. At one point, Eldredge begins to recount how God would give certain men in the Bible a new name before using them in mighty ways. He then went on to tell his own personal story about how, at a moment when he wasn't sure if he was doing with his life what God would have him do, God spoke to him in a profound and amazing way, giving him a new name that defined his work and purpose in life.

I have to admit that I was skeptical. I thought he was just employing some good writing techniques, some good ol' fashioned story tellin', in order to make his point and draw in the reader. But, as much as I was trying to resist his story, it was drawing *me* in. It was confronting and challenging my skepticism. So smiling, shaking my head, and staring out at the ocean, I decided that I was going to take a walk on the beach to see if God had a name for me too. Little did I know that the footprints I left in the sand behind me were the footprints of the *man* I was about to leave behind.

People who know me know that I am a talker, so being quiet long enough to listen to God was going to be a challenge. I guess that's how it is for each of us when it comes to our relationship with God. We are talkers. We rarely listen because the silence is too uncomfortable for many of us, and we are just too impatient to wait on an answer. On this particular day, I decided I would ask God a question and then be quiet and listen.

"God, do you have a name for me?" I humbly asked.

I waited, not expecting to hear anything but the sounds of children playing in the water with their parents. But before I even had a chance to clear my mind, a voice that sounded like a peal of thunder and a crashing wave shouted, "Nehemiah!!!"

The hair stood up on the back of my neck as I could hardly believe what I had just heard. It was so unbelievable to me that I immediately doubted it and tried to explain it away, but I knew what I had just heard. The cool guy in me thought, why on earth would I imagine hearing a name as lame as Nehemiah? I had no idea who this Nehemiah was, but I was certain that if I had fabricated the name I would have picked a much cooler name. My shame for second-guessing the most unbelievable moment of my life was outweighed by the lingering skeptic who would not, *could not*, believe what he had just heard. My doubt, and the skeptic, needed more proof.

"God, I am sorry that I am going to ask again, but do you have…"

"NEHEMIAH!!!"

I thought my world and everything around me had just stopped. I may have even peed my pants. I ran at a full sprint through the sand, straight to the condo, and up the stairs directly into our room. I didn't talk to my wife or my kids. I just sat down in front of my computer to find out about this Nehemiah. As I typed in the name and began to read, tears began to fill my eyes.

Nehemiah was a man in the Old Testament who was heartbroken for his people, the Jewish people. The Jews were to be God's holy, chosen people. They were to be God's image-bearers in the world. They were to be a blessing to all the nations. But, they had become a dishonor to God through their idolatrous and wicked ways. They had turned their back on God, on His Kingship, and His provision. Instead of being the people of the solution or the means through which God would work to bring and restore His righteousness, justice, and mercy in the world, they become part of the problem every step of the way.

As a result, Jerusalem became a disgrace before God. The wall that surrounded the city had been destroyed by Israel's enemies. The gates had been broken and ravaged by fire, and in this devastation the Jews living in Jerusalem were vulnerable to attack by their hostile enemies. The Golden Age in Israel was certainly gone and the people were a reproach in the sight of God.

That is what broke Nehemiah's heart. He knew who they were to be and what they had become instead. How could any of this ever be turned around? The problem of Jerusalem being in devastation, coupled with his people being a disgrace before Yahweh, seemed like a problem too monumental to ever turn be fixed. That is what Nehemiah wrestled with. That was his burden. And, to add to his frustration, he wasn't even in Jerusalem. He had a job working for the Persian king as a cupbearer. Not only was he far away from his people and from Jerusalem, he was in no position to do anything about the problem. Daily the burden weighed heavily on Nehemiah and he could not escape it. All he could do was pour himself out to God in fasting and prayer.

As I read the account of Nehemiah and his burden, tears continued to stream down my face. I knew how he felt on the inside. I knew the sadness and the burden that he had for his people and how they had become something very different than what God had always intended for them. I knew the feeling of the walls and gates being torn down, leaving the people vulnerable to attack. I knew what it was like to feel a thousand miles away and to realize that there was no way that a person in such a remote position could do anything to help or alleviate the problem. This is what I had been feeling for the last ten years and what broke my heart for the Church.

I see what the Church ought to be and what it has become. I see the figurative walls that have long crumbled down. I see the gates that have been burned. I see the enemies who have continued to invade while taking captive the people who are to be the means through which God ushers in the richness and fullness of His Kingdom on earth as it is in heaven. We, the people of God, stand behind the walls staring at the devastation of the Church. We who are to be the Body of Jesus Christ in the world are a fractured and divided mess. Some see the devastation and are heart-broken as well, but do not know what to do about it. Others look at the devastation and have become accustomed to it because they never knew it any other way. "The walls and gates are down", we say, "but what shall we do about it?"

While a burden will weigh on you, haunt you, and not leave you alone, what are you to do when you are in no position to do anything about it? What do you do when you see and hear about the devastation, yet it seems so far out of your control? What do you do when you are a nobody seemingly stuck in a distant land? How do you get to the place where the walls are torn down? What do you do when you don't have the right degrees and you find yourself working in a job that seems to be so far removed from the people and the broken wall? What more can you do but fast, pray, and cry out to God?

In Nehemiah, I saw myself. I was being changed from a man who had never even heard of Nehemiah to a man drawn to him, his burden for his people, and his faithfulness and resolve to seek God for a solution. It was this man, and his example, who was teaching me about the God who can and will move *how* He chooses and *when* He chooses. Nehemiah was a man of fasting and prayer, of seeking God's heart for his people, of crying out day and night for God to work and move in mighty and miraculous ways. It is in those moments that God moves in the most mysterious ways, using people that no one else would use and opening doors where no doors previously stood. But it is for His own purposes, not ours, that He works and moves in mighty ways. It is for His own glory, not ours, that He chooses whom He will choose and when.

The king saw the burden that Nehemiah carried and asked what it was that weighed him down. Though Nehemiah may have been fearful to tell the king of his burden, for it may have displeased him, he poured his heart out about his people and their devastation. Upon hearing the emotional cry of his servant, the king honored Nehemiah by sending him to Jerusalem accompanied with written documentation from the king, officers from the king's army, and enough money from the treasury to rebuild the walls of Jerusalem.

While Nehemiah may not have had all of the skill needed to rebuild the wall all by himself, he had assessed the situation by night and then began to tell the people about the work that needed to be done by day. Despite the opposition of a few people, the others began to rebuild the wall. It wasn't just one group of people with certain skills; it was a diverse group with a wide-array of skills who began to rebuild the wall and return to a position of honor before God. The crumbled walls were restored. The broken and devastated gates were replaced. God's people joined together as one, singing and praising the One who hears His people and their cries and who answers in His own way and in His own time.

This book is a result of my burden for the Church, what the Church has become, and *what it will soon come to be.* Let us rebuild our broken walls. Let us come together as one to do the work that needs to be done. Let us sing together the praises of the One who hears the cry of his Church and delivers her in His own way and His own time.

As I stand before each of you who read these words on these pages, I wonder what Nehemiah felt like when he finally stood before the people and began to address them. If he felt like I feel now, then he felt nervous, overwhelmed, and a little bit fearful. How will the people receive these words? Will they laugh and ignore the message? Will they ignore the messenger? Will people dismiss me because I am not a scholar or a pastor? Will they think that I am a smug or arrogant for saying these words? Will religious people fight for specific doctrines and positions while standing against the united Body of Christ? Will churches hold on to and cling to their consumer-driven approach rather embrace the sacrificial life of the Suffering Servant? The questions just do not end.

The truth is that I don't know much. I feel too tiny and insignificant to be used. I am well aware of my misgivings. I was even fearful of writing my Nehemiah story because I was afraid that you would think I am completely crazy (and maybe you do). But here is the thing…I don't have all the answers. I won't pretend to have everything figured out. There are people who are smarter than I. There are people who are better writers than I. And there are people who are even nicer than I. But all I have ever wanted was to be used by God, to help any way I can to rebuild the Church that is in disarray, and for God to receive the glory, the honor, and the praise for bringing these dead bones to life, breathing a fresh breath of the Spirit upon us, and giving us a new heart for embodying and extending His Kingdom on earth as it is in heaven. And it is to that end I press on.

Brandon Andress
September 2009

CHAPTER 1

THE TIME HAS COME

I have known for a while that I had to write this book because well-intentioned people have quieted a message once announced to the ages as the greatest news ever heard, hushing it to back room whispers. They have silenced this momentous announcement, the hope-filled call to the entire created order. And now, lesser messengers with lesser messages have replaced the universal Kingdom proclamation of freedom and liberation once shouted from the rooftops and shared in wild excitement from person to person in busy cities and towns around the world. The profound message of the Kingdom of God, the reason for which Jesus was sent to earth, has become but a faint whisper among the loud and empty choruses that fill the air and compete for attention in our churches.

Scattered throughout the centuries, a few men and women heard the whispered message of this Kingdom behind closed doors and were transformed in every aspect of their lives. The same people then made frantic attempts to reach the rooftops and proclaim it to others, only to find the streets cleared except for an occasional interested passerby. Many disinterested people have retreated back into their homes while others have been ushered into the great church palaces. The rooftop announcements of a new Kingdom and a new way of living have turned into echoes bouncing off of the seemingly impenetrable and mighty Church `walls.

It is time to come down from the rooftops. It is time to stop shouting the Kingdom message into the lonely streets. This message of the Kingdom of God must be heard by every person across the land and must break through the mighty Church walls so that every man, woman, and child can hear it clearly and understand it. The great announcement, the hope-filled call to the created order, the universal proclamation is breaking through the walls of the mighty Church palace and is thundering like a deafening, crashing wave and it cannot be silenced. The message of the Kingdom of God is here and it must be heard by all!

This message of the Kingdom of God is one for the common man and the common woman. It is an announcement for the rich and poor, the slave and free. It is a proclamation for the kings and queens, the presidents and magistrates, the subjects and the peasants. It is a call to the African, Asian, European, American, to each and every race, nation, tribe, and tongue. It is the great emancipation proclamation for those within the religious institutions and denominations, inviting the Baptist, the Methodist, the Lutheran, the Catholic, the conservative, the liberal, and every single man, woman, and child who call Jesus as Lord out of division and into unity. It is the greatest clarion call in history for humanity and an irresistible beckoning call for peace and justice, forgiveness and mercy, reconciliation and unity, and above all else, love. If you have ears, you must hear. The time has come to hear about the Kingdom of God!

The World is Ready

Humanity has never been more ready for such a great and transformative message to break into our world and be embodied in thought, action, and deed. We have been looking for and trusting those things that we can see, but are just now starting to realize that *those* things fail and do not last. We have put too much faith and trust in our governments and leaders and have come to realize they are full of promises that fail us and that are never delivered upon. We mistakenly look to them for freedom and find ourselves oppressed...and even more, depressed. We trust in their moral judgment and character, yet we move from headline to headline of moral failure, infidelity, and special interest. The cycle never ends. It continues over and over and over. From year to year, from decade to decade, from century to century, the cycle continues.

We continue to entrust those who can't be trusted, and empower those who take power from the already powerless. We become cynical and jaded, wondering if anything at all deserves our faith and trust. We have become the cynics and the skeptics, questioning every system and power structure, every politician and every leader, but we are prone to folly and easily fall prey to the next talking-head offering sweet lip-service.

Our stupor and fancy fades and comes crashing back to reality as we become more embittered and encrusted than we have ever been. We look around the globe and see nation after nation and government after government in disarray and in the midst of upheaval. People are struggling and rising up within their countries against tyranny and oppression because we intuitively know that there *is* such a thing as justice, yet it always seems to slip through our fingertips.

Ironically, our money and economies are just as uncertain as our leaders and our governments. The financial powerbrokers loan and invest money in order to make more money on the backs of the lowest income earners. And, when the schemes fall short, they reach behind the backs of the distracted, hard-working wage earner and pull more money out of his pockets.

Nations float belly up because their currencies are worthless. States warn that they are out of money. Unemployment continues to rise with no end in sight. Nations continue to borrow into oblivion, not just on the backs of the oppressed wage earner but now on the backs of our children and grandchildren.

State cries out to the nation. The nation cries out to other nations. We stand witness to nations suffering through their own internal struggles, while the down-trodden and weary populace hopes and prays there will be another country or leader who will come to the rescue, but it never seems to materialize. We all just sit on the brink, wondering if this is really what it is all about. Seriously, is this what it is all about?

If we have not had enough internal struggles, we are certainly having our fill of external struggles. Countries are threatening other countries. Nations are fighting against other nations. Kingdoms are rising up and aligning with each other against threats, enemies, and other aggressors. It is impossible to escape the minute-by-minute news coverage that is littered with threats and the possibilities of war, as if to remind us that the pursuit of peace can only come at the cost of human life. To that end, we war on. There is not a day that goes by without another bombing or missile test. Weapons arsenals are built up, uranium is enriched, and the world continues to watch and wait anxiously, still longing for justice and now wondering if we will ever experience world peace.

While the nations stockpile weapons and spend trillions of dollars every year to maintain and improve upon their weaponry, nearly a billion people around the globe are hungry. Even more indicting is the fact that every day about 16,000 children die from starvation. We create weapons to keep our "enemies" from killing people, yet we are comfortable letting 16,000 children die every day (one every five seconds)![1]

But it isn't just the lack of food and water, it is the absence of sustainable life and the increasing number of people globally who are severely poverty-stricken and ravaged by disease. The wealthiest people and nations in the world have the means to eradicate hunger, poverty, and disease, yet in the lap of luxury the problems of the world seem like trivial inconveniences. Ironically, governments and world bodies promise to eradicate these problems, yet the problems only seem to get worse. The world is upside-down in all the wrong ways, and we wonder if there is any reason to have hope.

There are so many ways to describe the way we feel about what is happening in the world. One could say the pressure continues to build like a heart attack waiting to happen. It is palpable and we can feel it coming on. Another could say that we have a strange and uneasy feeling in our collective gut. The world seems to be wildly out of control and we can feel it churning. Even another might say it is like a pregnant woman whose birth pains and contractions continue to increase from week to week and then from day to day, until the labor pain no longer pauses. You feel the contractions. You feel the pain. You know that something is coming. No matter where you are in the world, or how you describe it, it seems to all of us as if we are careening into a future in which we hardly know what to do or where to turn.

We have turned away from those who ought to help us make sense of this upside-down world. In our churches, we have found an identity crisis which has led to an untransformed people who lack purpose in our communities and in the larger world. Our churches profess to have all the answers, but we are untransformed in our living, looking no different than those who aren't a part of the Church. Sadly enough, we seem to be more concerned about being the means to our own end rather than a part of the solution. This, many times, takes on the form of self-interested pursuits *in* the Church rather than the form of selfless pursuits *through* the Church.

That is not to say that there are not amazing and godly followers of Jesus scattered throughout our churches, who are the very hands and feet of Christ in the world. But we would be amiss not to recognize the great problem of the Church in the world. The Church has lost its true identity and purpose in and for the world, and we do not even know where to begin looking to regain our identity and purpose. We are like the proverbial dog chasing its tail, but never quite able to catch it. The Church does not recognize that the things we foolishly chase around in circles are not the things we need in the first place, and they are certainly not the things in which a lost and cynical world will find hope, faith, and trust.

So where in the world do we turn for help? Do we turn to our political and religious leaders who are nothing more than human beings themselves, prone to error, mistake, and missing the point? Do we turn to our governments who continue to take more power and liberty from the individual while confusing freedom for oppression? Do we look to other nations and other leaders and pray that somehow, someway, someone has the answers and solutions, only to have the rug pulled out from under us again? Do we turn back to the judgmental and superficial religious institutions that have lost relevance because of their commercialism, apathy, judgmentalism, and hypocrisy? Do we turn to the same people, institutions, bureaucracies, and governments who have been responsible for the global inequities, crises, and problems that we face? To whom *do* we turn?

The questions we ask are age old questions. Every generation has experienced the cyclical pattern of human triumph and failure. It is in the times of our greatest failure to each other that we begin to wonder what it is all about and how it all ends. When we long for justice, when we seek peace, when all we have is hope, we wonder where we ought to look to find the answer. When it seems as if the light passing from the sun to earth is slowly being eclipsed and then blocked by the moon, we stand in darkness and wonder when the eclipse will end and the light will finally break through again.

A great light is finally breaking through into the darkness. For what was hidden and lost in the darkness has now been exposed to the light and found. The great treasure that had been buried under a mound of earth for so long in a desolate field has been discovered and purchased and is now ready to be shared with the world. The one thing which will give the Church identity and purpose has been found. We stand together on this ground with shovels in hand ready to unearth and reclaim the great and transformative message of the Kingdom of God that has been buried for far too long, and the world waits in eager anticipation for the riches of this Kingdom to be revealed.

Again, a wondrous pearl of the greatest and highest value that had been lost in a pile of lesser trinkets and cheap jewelry has been found and purchased by a generous merchant. He is setting it richly in preparation for the Great Marriage of the Bride and Bridegroom. The King is sending his messengers to deliver the invitations and the banquet hall doors are opening wide as all of creation waits with eager expectation to sing a new song in one accord.

So come down from the rooftops and let all of the created order hear your voices! Open wide the mighty Church palace doors and fill the streets! Run into the neighborhoods and wake those who have been sleeping! Wake up sleepers, arise! Flood the highways, the byways, the alleyways and proclaim, "The time has come! The time has come! The Kingdom of God has come near! Be transformed and believe this great news of Jesus Christ that was once hidden but has now been found!"

CHAPTER 2

EYES TO SEE AND EARS TO HEAR

The Church is like an adopted son who tells his father how much he loves him and how much he wants to make him proud, but then ignores the important things his father asks of him day after day. When the father finally confronts his son on the important matters that have been continually neglected, the son replies, "But father, do I not tell you how much I love you? Do I not I tell you how wonderful you are?"

"You do son," the father replies, "but even though you continue to tell me how much you love me and how wonderful of a father I am because of my example, you continue to ignore my requests and remain untransformed in your life. Have I not asked you to change your ways and follow my example? Have I not asked you to be an example in our community by the way you live? Have I not asked you to feed those in our community who are hungry? Have I not asked you to help the homeless find a place to stay? Have I not asked over and over for you to give to those in need, to help those who are sick, to visit those who are imprisoned? But time after time you ignore my requests. So how can you truly say you love me and seek to make me proud, when you do not do what I ask of you?"

Listless and embarrassed, the son just stares at the ground.

But the father continues, "Can we not reason together? Or will you continue to follow the way of your older brother? I could not stand it when he would bring gifts to me, have celebrations for me, make requests of me, and then ignore the important things that I requested of him. So I finally cut him off and have been waiting for him to come to his senses. Do you think I will not cut you off as well? You ignore my requests and you are arrogant about it. So please, until you are ready to change, stop with the empty words, the gifts, the celebrations, and the requests and empty praise because they are detestable. Change the way you live your life. Stop doing wrong and learn to do right! Learn how to seek justice and encourage those who cannot defend themselves. Defend the little ones who do not have parents. Care for the widows in our town and plead their case for them. If these matters are important to me, should they not be important to you as well?"[2]

Jesus and Religion

The harshest words of Jesus were, *and continue to be*, directed at those like the adopted son, who offer their love and adoration toward God the Father but remain untransformed in their living and neglect the important matters that the Father expects from them. They are the people who say all the right things about God, go through all the right motions, give their gifts of sacrifice and praise to God, and have weekly ceremonies in honor of God, but who live unchanged lives and ignore who God wants them to be in the world. Ironically, they have followed the wayward path of Israel that the prophets warned so much about. The people of God profess Him with their lips but profane Him among the nations by neglecting His ways.

So it should not be surprising to us that there will be those who call on the name of the Lord but who will be called cursed. Make note, it is not I who says they will be cursed; it is Jesus.[3] For the religious are those who profess their faith with their lips but live untransformed in their lives. They attend church services but look like the world in their actions. They say their prayers to God but ignore the requests of the weak. They give their money but neglect the cause of the poor.

I could list countless examples of how I have seen this play out in churches over the last few years, but the objective of this book is not to point out the speck in one person's eye while ignoring the log that has been jammed in my face for so long. The objective of this book is to open our eyes to the life and world altering reality of the Kingdom of God and to demonstrate how it can transform us, individually and as the Church, to move forward in unity for the sake of the world, becoming all that God intended us to be by following the way of Jesus through the power of the Holy Spirit. However, I have noticed that it is difficult for people to understand exactly what I am talking about if I do not give a few examples.

I was contacted by a high school senior who was working on a senior project for graduation. She told me that she wanted to work with churches in order to fully stock and supply the local domestic abuse shelter for women. After asking her a few questions about her plan and telling her that we were definitely in, I asked if she had already contacted other churches to get their support. She told me that she had a list of five churches and had already contacted four of them; we were the fifth. Three of the churches told her no, and one church said they would have to take it to their elders and get back with her, which they did and ultimately said no.

I felt so frustrated and ashamed. How difficult is it for a church to set out a box to collect supplies and then make an announcement about it? Little did I know that the story was about to get worse. I asked the senior what church she attended. She said, "I don't go to church. But in my project planning I just thought the people most likely to help with a project like this would be people in the church. I have been really surprised at their unwillingness to help."

What could I say to her? Absolutely nothing.

Too many times we create rules and protocols in our churches that we believe must be followed. We get so fixated on the rules and laws we make that we miss the larger point of who we are to be and what we are to be doing in the lives of people in our communities and in the larger world. We miss the fullness and richness of living and embodying the Gospel. Here is another story to illustrate my point.

One early Sunday morning as I and a couple of friends were hanging out at our church building a man walked in and told me that the heater went out in his apartment. He explained that his family was huddled together under one single blanket in the frigid, single-digit apartment. He went to the local homeless shelter in to see if he could get a portable heater and blankets. The shelter gave the man a name of a local church where he could go to in order to get help. The man walked over to the church, went inside, and began telling people about his situation. To his surprise, the answer that he was given on this Sunday morning was, "Our office is closed and we are unable to get a check, so we cannot help."

Now granted, he may have just talked to the wrong people and it is possible that if he had spoken to someone else the result may have been different, but in my experience, situations like this are not uncommon in our churches. That leads to a great irony: we show up to worship our

God, to sing His praises, and to learn how to be like Him, but we have difficulty connecting our affinity toward God to real life and, as a result, are negligent in recognizing our identity and the purpose God has given us as the Church in the world.

We, too many times, miss the forest for the trees. We are not quite sure what the point of our faith is beyond our own individual salvation. We are quite good at understanding that "Jesus died for our sins and that our sins have been forgiven," but we are not quite sure what to do about it…other than "be a good person and wait for heaven."

For instance, there is a guy from a church in my city who said, "Our church is not in the business of helping the homeless." The crazy thing about it is…I believe him! His church is *not* in the business of helping the homeless, but as followers of Christ, *we all should be, right?* The Scripture reminds us of the words of Jesus when he said, "For what you have done to the least of these, you have done also to me." Those pushed to the edges of society ought to be the concern of the Christian. Ironically, I have found that several important Christian leaders in my town did not realize that we have a homeless shelter. How can we take seriously the call to care for the "least of these" when we have convinced ourselves that helping the poor is not *our business*? Are we not to put our faith into practice in real and tangible ways? Do our salvation and the empowering of the Holy Spirit not propel us to *live and act differently* for God's purposes in the world? Does God not expect anything more from us than "being good people" as we "wait for heaven?"

We have so watered down the richness and robustness of our faith that it has come mostly to represent the task of "saving people's souls." As a result we have come to believe that the message of the Gospel does not have much real practical application for the individual and the Church beyond that. In essence, the Gospel is good for my individual salvation, but it means very little for the transforming and healing work that God wants to do in the world through his saved people.

For instance, there have been several people who have asked my opinion of local churches in town spending millions of dollars on new church buildings. In response I have said, "Man, the drug and substance abuse problem is getting really bad downtown and it is really negatively affecting families and children. Wouldn't it would be awesome to use some of that money and manpower to create an intensive drug and substance abuse program organized by prayerful Christians who God could use to help free those who are addicted and enslaved by drugs?" And to my surprise, the Christians respond by saying, "Why would we do that? What does *that* have to do with the Gospel? Why is *that* the responsibility of the Church?"

These are just a few examples out of many that show our narrow view and understanding of the Gospel. We have a misaligned idea of how the Gospel of Jesus Christ relates to the identity and task of the Christian in the community and world. Even more, it highlights how disconnected our idea of the Gospel is from practical application. I know this disconnect is not happening in just one church or in one town. It is epidemic throughout the Church as a whole. I know people. I talk to people. I see what we are doing in the Church. It is obvious that we have been and continue to be negligent in our application of the Gospel to real life, in taking it beyond a mental thing and letting it transform us from the inside-out of our own lives and then into action. *I am pointing the finger back at myself more than anyone else, as I have missed the point too many times in my life to count.* We have so isolated and insulated ourselves that, not only have we turned a blind eye to how we might be able to help the very least in our midst, we have insured that there is no way for us to develop any kind of real and meaningful relationship with them. Don't miss my point. I am not suggesting that we have to be doing something for someone each moment of the day. However, I am suggesting that we are significantly lacking in a love that breaks out from our lives and touches the people in our towns and cities. We are a people who care significantly more about our own interests than the interests of those who desperately need the love and compassion of Christ lived out through our lives. This negligence is absolutely tragic and I will be the first one in line asking God to forgive me for missing the point.

We have been caught in, and have a very difficult time escaping, the trappings of religion, even though we may feel as if we are really well-intentioned in what we do. If the Church is ever going to find its heart, its soul, its first love, then it will have to finally break away from religion, pettiness, and shallow, superficial, self-centered living in order to [re]discover our identity in Jesus Christ and the selfless, loving, and sacrificial way of the Kingdom of God. The Church must become the meek, humble, contrite, and lowly suffering servant to the world. But, it is only when we discover the Kingdom of God that we will find our identity and purpose, and then the Power needed to begin transforming the world.

Religion

It is absolutely critical to understand that the Kingdom of God stands in stark contrast to the ways, workings, and thinking of the religious. Jesus and religion have never mixed. Unfortunately the Church, or the means through which the Kingdom of God *ought* to be proclaimed and demonstrated to the world, has become overwhelmingly compromised by religion and religious people, well-intentioned or not, who have buried deep the treasure of the Kingdom of God. We will begin to better understand what the Kingdom of God is and why it is essential for the follower of Christ in short order, but we must first look inward at the way religion has kept this vital message from the eyes, ears, and heart of the Church.

The pursuits of religion are like weeds that choke the vine of the Kingdom of God and keep it from producing fruit.[4] In the absence of fruit produced by a life centered on the Kingdom of God, we find apathy, self-centered pursuits, and superficiality. In fact, the weeds of religion are exactly opposite of the abundant fruit of the Kingdom of God. Religion may look good on the outside, but it is spiritually empty on the inside. It is like a cup that looks clean and shiny on the outside, but upon closer examination it is filthy and unusable on the inside.[5] Religion may even resemble a tomb that has been scrubbed, washed, and cleaned on the outside but is full of death, bones, and everything unclean on the inside.[6] Religion always has a good appearance on the outside, but is dead and void on the inside.

The religious go to a church service on Sunday, wear the right clothes, say the right words, have all the "church" answers, go through the right motions and have an endless number of traditions, but are reluctant to follow the way of Jesus in their lives. The religious are in desperate need of the Spirit of God who could break into the hollowness and shallowness of their lives to produce a radical and sacrificial discipleship that further breaks out in love producing right-living, justice, and mercy for the entire world to see.

Religion keeps one on the periphery of life, walking around in circles blindly, and keeps the Spirit of God from breaking through the surface to transform the heart. No matter how ornate, decorated, and well-meaning religion is on the outside, it is absolutely worthless if it does not bring a person to full life-transformation from the inside out.

Church Lover

Now, before I go way too far too fast, let me tell you who I am. I am a fanatical lover of the Church and one who obsesses over what the Church should be in the world. I no more enjoy pointing out the inadequacies, failures, and hypocrisies of the Church than I enjoy getting a tooth drilled, but it is necessary that we come to terms with and begin discussing the truth of the situation in which we find ourselves. I don't think for a second that everyone in the Church is bad. In fact, there are many individuals within the Church who are living Spirit-filled Kingdom-centered lives every moment of the day! But I believe it is a small number in comparison to the whole.

I also believe it is our leadership within the churches that is primarily to blame for the state of the Church, for its waywardness, for its lack of depth, for its superficiality, for its blindness, and for its religiosity. For it is behind *our* leadership that the people follow, and we, the shepherds, have not led well. It is our responsibility to feed, nurture, and protect those in our care. It is our responsibility to nurse those who are sick back to health. It is our responsibility to help those in our care to have the eyes to see and the ears that hear the Truth of God, but we ourselves must have the eyes to see and the ears to hear first. So shall the blind continue to lead the blind? Or shall the light finally break through into the darkness that we may all see?

We have long looked for light but what we have seen is darkness. We have long sought after the brightness, but we have continued to walk in the shadows. We have long been like blind people feeling our way along the wall stumbling about, but the light is beginning to break into the darkness.[7] The people who have been walking in this darkness will see the great light. And this light will reveal that which has been hidden for far too long.

I believe the brightest and most revolutionary days of the Church are in our midst, but they will only begin when we finally have the eyes to see that the Church is the means through which the Kingdom of God will be embodied and announced to the entire created order! For if it is not the Church who will be the light in the growing darkness of the world then who will it be? It is for this realization I work and I ask you to join me.

13

Kingdom of God and Fluff

As I mentioned earlier, the Church has been compromised by religion, which has choked out the Kingdom of God. The great riches of the Kingdom of God have been buried deep in the metaphorical ground. As a result, the purpose and identity of the Church have been replaced with various false purposes and identities. The perception of the Church by many in our communities is that it has become a superficial, mass-marketed, fluff and puff, demographic-driven, entertainment organization or a stiff, rigid, legalistic, overly-political, and judgmental organization that seems to exist for its own purposes. *Neither description of the Church is the embodiment of the Kingdom of God, nor is it what the Church ought to be or how the Church ought to be viewed in the world.*

The Kingdom of God should never be confused with "seeker sensitive services," slick ways to impress or recruit people to join the club, or a "relevant" marketing ploy or gimmick. The Kingdom of God does not need to be watered down, dressed up, or hyped-up in order to move in power and invite a desperate and hungry world into complete transformation. Furthermore, the Kingdom of God is not a rigid, stiff, legalistic, oppressive, political, or judgmental movement. It does not judge or condemn the world. It does not move out in hate and anger. And it certainly does not abuse, fracture, break, or tear down individuals, families, churches, communities, countries, or the world.

Rather, the Kingdom of God is the most revolutionary, stand-alone, in-your-face reality in the history of humankind! It is the most liberating, loving, and restoring movement that has ever been initiated for the world to see and for the world to join. It is the most merciful and grace-filled movement that has ever been witnessed, demonstrating through our lives the best and highest ways of God for the healing of the nations.

The sad reality is that the Church, in its blindness, deafness, and maybe even deadness, has been sorely ignorant of and cannot seem to find the beautiful realities of this Kingdom announced and embodied by Jesus Christ. It is this very reality that has led the Church into the metaphorical desert, walking around in circles, fighting and complaining, while continuing to *neglect its identity, purpose, and calling for the world in and through Jesus Christ.*

The late Messianic Jewish author, Arthur Katz, said it this way about the current state of the Church:

> The thing that mutilates us as the church is our inveterate,

stick-in-the-mud, ego-centrism. We bring into the church the same mind-set that we had in the world, by which *we* continue to be at the center. Is that not why we have so many problems? We measure ourselves by ourselves, by how much we like the services, the worship, the preaching. Everything is still predicated on what *we* like and what pleases *us*. And if we do not like it, we move to another fellowship. Everything is seen in terms of *our* satisfaction, *our* pleasure. That mindset is death! But, praise God, He has given us a purpose that is beyond ourselves, that has not ourselves as the end purpose. The purposes of God are the means to an end larger and other than ourselves by which, when we give ourselves to it, we come into true fulfillment of ourselves.[8]

The Church is to be a means used by God for an end larger than ourselves. We give ourselves sacrificially to it. We become less and God becomes more. It is all about God's will and God's way in our lives and in the life of the Church. The purpose for which we have been called by Jesus is to be the embodiment of the Kingdom of God in the world and for the world. Our purpose is to extend the Kingdom of God throughout the world in the hearts and minds of those who come to believe as a result of the way God has worked through us as the unified Body of Christ. But we have become so ego-centric and so self-focused that we have become something very different than what God intended. And to that end, the Church has come to be perceived as nothing close to the Christ that it professes to follow.

Perceptions of the Church

If you are worried that I have gone too far in my short assessment of religion and the Church, please know that there is a wealth of anecdotes and data that supports my claims. There are generations of people who have been turned off by the Church, many of whom actually grew up in the Church. The number of people joining our churches in the United States continues to dwindle decade after decade, losing relevance in the daily affairs of the world. One of the main reasons for the continuing decline is the negative perception of the Church by various generational groups outside of the Church, especially young adults. For these groups,

Christians are primarily viewed as hypocritical, too focused on getting converts, anti-homosexual, sheltered, too political, and judgmental.

Granted, this is a very broad stroke of the brush, but perception is reality for those who are doing the perceiving. The perceptions people have of the Church come in a variety of ways from first-hand experience, information from other sources, and other painful encounters and hurtful experiences from Christians.[9] Consequently, the Church continues to lose relevance in a world that quickly dismisses it in perceived, or real, hypocrisy. The Church preaches one thing, yet many of those who identify themselves with the Church live untransformed lives. To the world, the Church has become a group of holier-than-thou individuals who claim a certain special status, but look, act, and behave like everyone else. Our team looks pretty good from the inside, but from the outside there is very little that seems appealing based on the life of the Christian and the Church.

On many fronts, from divorce rates to gambling and from pornography to serving in the community, the Church looks no different than the larger culture. The term Christian has become more of a label indicating that a person identifies with a single church rather than one who has taken up the cross of Christ, died to the old ways of the world, and is continuously transformed in power by the working of the Spirit of God to look and act like Jesus Christ in the world every moment of the day.

With the Church preaching one way of life and living another, it is no wonder that the people of the world find it easier to ignore God and just try to be good people without the hassle of the Church. We are largely responsible for repelling people away from God by the way we have represented God in the world in our individual lives and in our churches. To the world, we have lost our voice and any inkling of relevance. That is why so many generations, most especially young people, are turning away from the Church and pursuing agnosticism, atheism, universalism, and activism.

Identity and Purpose

When relevance is lost, one begins searching wildly to find an identity and a purpose. That is exactly what the Church has done. Ironically, the *only* thing that can give the Church identity and purpose, the Kingdom of God, has long been buried. The Church, unable to see what it is missing and what it desperately needs, has tried in vain attempt after vain attempt to find a tactic or ploy that will give it identity and purpose. We have watched as church after church runs around in circles trying to figure out what will get people to come in through the doors. The Church has come to resemble a business trying to figure out the wants, needs, and desires of the consumers rather than rather simply becoming the Body of Christ in the world by extending the Kingdom of God in its streets and neighborhoods.

The church pours time, energy, effort, and resources into making the centralized Sunday worship service "the event" or something new and relevant so as to retain the people it has and to attract people from whom it has become so disconnected. Churches have created program after program and service after service trying to find the one thing that will "work." The problem is that when the hype, glitz, and glam wears away, it is still searching for something to fill the void and something for which the people of the world want to give their lives.

No matter how clean or beautifully decorated the tomb is, it still has the same thing on the inside. We do not need more decoration. We need internal cleansing. We need a purpose larger than ourselves that will eclipse the self-centered, ego-centrism that has divided and crippled us for far too long. The larger purpose that will unite the Church and give it an identity and mission in the world is the central and most important message of Jesus Christ, the Kingdom of God, nothing more and nothing less.

Is This Shocking?

So depending on who you are, this is either shocking news or a huge sigh of relief. Either it shocks you, like it once did me, because you would have never believed that you could be involved in church *and* be completely missing the most important, monumental, and revolutionary reality that has ever existed, while continuing to spin your wheels in fruitless endeavors looking for identity, purpose, and something that sticks. Or, this news gives you a sigh of relief because you have always known that there had to be more than what you and your church settled for, yet you just didn't know where to go or where to look. Either way, I hope that this clarification compels you to curiosity and hunger, and pushes you further into your own individual pursuit of the treasure that has been hidden for so long.

Just so we are clear from the outset, I am pouring my heart and soul out to those of you who have not realized until now how broken, dysfunctional, and misaligned we are as a group of people who proclaim to follow Christ. I am pouring my heart and soul out to those of you who do not know what the Kingdom of God is, and to those of you who did not realize that the Kingdom of God is the identity and purpose of the Church. I am pouring my heart and soul out to those of you who have perpetuated a religious system, willingly or unwillingly. I am pouring my heart and soul out to those of you who hold on tightly to power, control, and politics within your churches.

I am pouring my heart and soul out to those of you who have commercialized Jesus and your churches in order to attract and entertain people who are hungry to consume. I am pouring my heart and soul out to each one of you who have been living inside of the torn down and devastated walls and have been there so long that you haven't even noticed the problems. I beg of you, please see the problems. Honestly look at yourself and your church as you read the following pages. Let the Truth of Christ pierce your heart and awaken your Spirit to the Kingdom of God.

The Kingdom Lost

Over the last few years I have spent an enormous amount of time speaking with those within the Church about the Kingdom of God and have been surprised at how few even know what it is. Despite it being the primary message of Jesus in the Gospels, mentioned over 120 times in His teachings and parables, many Christians are ignorant of its meaning and importance. How is it that we can read the Gospels and hear the message of Jesus taught day after day, yet not know or understand His most central message? How is it that Jesus can mention a particular phrase over 120 times, yet we fail to discuss it? How is it that virtually every parable of Jesus begins with, "The Kingdom of God is like…" yet we never ask what the Kingdom of God even is? We certainly have our work cut out for us if we are to discover the richness of Jesus' primary message.

My hope is that we can walk together through the words and parables of Christ to uncover the Kingdom of God, understand it clearly, and then put it into practice in our own lives and in the life of the Church. But in order to do this, we will need to bring together several parables and stories of Jesus, and then begin to weave them together into a larger Kingdom tapestry for each of us to see more clearly. Through our journey, we will begin to see that the parables we have studied and viewed in isolation for so long are, in fact, a beautifully woven tapestry that brings the Kingdom message of Jesus to the very forefront and gives us a new identity and purpose for which we are called as the Church for the sake of the world.

Seeds and Soil

When Jesus spoke to his followers in parables, or short stories that make a moral point, he would not always explain the meaning of the parable. Many times, this would leave the audience wondering and talking about it. They would try to figure out who they were in the story and what lesson they could learn from it. Sometimes people got it, sometimes they didn't.

So while Jesus used images and common situations in his parables and teachings that people could understand and easily relate to, the hidden truth or meaning was not always obvious to the audience. Even though Jesus would sometimes explain His parables to His disciples, they were curious why He would not always explain the same parables to the larger audience. This was exactly the case with one particular parable that stopped the crowd in their tracks and left them wondering what exactly Jesus meant without receiving any sort of explanation. It was the story of the seed sower.[10] Here is a paraphrase of that parable.

Early one morning, a farmer got up before sunrise, got dressed, and went out to his shed to prepare for his day in the field. It wasn't a large field at all, but it wasn't small either. It was too small to use the heavy farming equipment, but almost too large to do the work by hand. Either way, the farmer loved the field and the work and enjoyed getting out early while the dew was still on the ground. It was the perfect time of season to cultivate the land and begin planting seeds.

As the farmer finished hoeing most of the field, he picked up his large bag of seed and began walking the rows and scattering seed in the newly worked areas. As a good farmer, he knew that sowing seeds in the right soil conditions and at the right depth were both important for the plants to get the right nourishment in order to take root and grow big. But he was also very liberal about sowing his seeds and his method wasn't understood by those close to him. His approach to sowing seed always confused those who would ask him how he did it. He would just walk the rows and toss seed here and toss seed there. It was a little funny and quite unorthodox, but it always seemed to produce a good crop in those places where the seeds took root.

It wasn't uncommon to walk around the field and see birds eating what was tossed and left on top of the ground. Birds would swoop in, land, and devour the seeds. Those seeds never even had a chance of taking root and growing. They were gone as quickly as they were sown, and the birds seemed satisfied.

Some of the other seeds landed in rocky areas on top of the soil that were hidden from the birds. To those who didn't pay close attention, it may have surprised them to see the seeds come to life so quickly. Within days the seeds near the rocks were breaking forth to the heavens, but just as quickly withering and dying because they did not take root or receive enough nourishment and water. This always left everyone a little sad and disappointed that something with so much potential would just wither away so quickly.

The same thing could be said for the seeds that were planted in shallow ground. The little seedling would break through the soil beaming toward the radiant sun only to shrivel away into nothing. It was the same story over and over for the seeds that were planted in the shallow ground.

If it was not the seed that was falling among the rocks or landing in shallow soil that withered away, it was the seed landing on the edge of the field near the weeds and thorn bushes that was choked to death. The seedlings would begin to take root and stand tall on the edge of the field, and then the weeds and thorn bushes would begin to choke the life out of them. The seedlings never stood a chance against the overpowering weeds and thorns.

But this was the way of the farmer, sowing and scattering a lot of seeds all throughout the field. While some of the seeds would get eaten quickly or would never take root, the seeds that found a home deep within the nourishing soil, protected from the harsh elements, would grow and thrive and produce a great abundance of crop. The farmer always produced more than what anyone expected.

For an audience that understood quite well the ins and outs of farming, this made perfect practical sense. You sow the seeds deep within the nourishing soil so it can take root and grow abundantly. It doesn't work out so well when you sow seeds on top of the soil so birds can eat them, in shallow soil that will cause the seedling to wither away, or even near the weeds that choke the life out of the seedling.

It was parables such as this one that had meaning that wasn't always obvious or apparent to everyone who heard it. Many in the audience may have appreciated the interesting story from Jesus about things they could relate to, but many had *no idea* about the deeper truth He was teaching them. They could see and hear what was right in front of them, but were blind and deaf to the hidden treasure of which Jesus spoke. This is why the disciples were so confused when Jesus would not explain the parable to the audience because the audience did not understand the deeper truth of the parable.

The disciples very well may have been wondering why He chose to announce this Good News of the Kingdom of God in such puzzling and mysterious ways. *Why not just tell the people what You want to tell them so it is obvious?* Certainly a seeker friendly version would be a better approach so that the audience would easily understand it. Maybe even a fill-in-the-blank sermon would help them see and hear what Jesus was talking about. But Jesus responded to the disciples by saying, "The knowledge of the secrets of the Kingdom of God has been given to you and not them."

What?! How could Jesus say such an insulting thing about the audience? How could He be so comfortable *not* explaining *exactly* what He meant to convey to the people that day? If He wants people to understand His mission and message and wants people to join Him, then why doesn't He take time to explain His story? How will His audience grow? How will His Kingdom message get out?!

Jesus' callous statement about the audience may seem confusing when read out of context, but when Jesus continues, His point becomes much clearer:

Though seeing, they do not see;
   though hearing, they do not hear or understand.

In them is fulfilled the prophecy of Isaiah:

You will be ever hearing but never understanding;
   you will be ever seeing but never perceiving.

For this people's heart has become calloused;
they hardly hear with their ears, and they have closed their eyes.

Otherwise they might see with their eyes,
   hear with their ears, understand with their hearts
   and turn, and I would heal them. Matthew 13:13-15

The people in the audience that day did not have the eyes to see or the ears to hear the deeper truth of which Jesus spoke. The hearts of the people had become callous and, as a result, He did not feel compelled to explain it to them. While it is true that Jesus was referring specifically to the audience who had been following him around, for even if he *had* explained his parable to them they would not be able to see or hear the deeper meaning, we can be certain that "missing the point" is not a unique phenomenon to only the first century Jewish audience. In fact, it is quite possible for *any* person, even the most well-intentioned, to walk through life as a sleepwalker, a person with eyes and ears who is living and breathing, but who is dead to their identity and purpose in God. Sleepwalkers are those who are unable to see and hear the Truth of God clearly, even though it is presented clearly to them. We may read and hear the Scriptures a thousand times over, but we may still not understand how they are meant for our lives. We can't see it. We can't hear it. Our hearts have become callous to the deeper truth of Christ. When we live in this way *we* are the sleepwalkers. We are dead to the true realities of the world.

It is to such people the Scriptures proclaim, "Wake up, O sleeper, rise from the dead and Christ will shine on you."[11] Open your eyes! Open your ears! Take off the blinders! Open the fertile soil of your heart to receive the Kingdom seed that Jesus is planting deep!

That is why, when we read accounts of Jesus not explaining the parable to the crowd, we may be wise to ask ourselves who *we* are in the story and what *we* can learn from it. Are we *the disciples* or *the audience* listening to this parable of Jesus? Could it be that we are the people hearing the parable but missing the point? Or do we too often assume, without putting much thought into it, that we are like the disciples getting the inside scoop from Jesus?

My observation is that we, in the Church, believe too often that we are the "insiders" with special knowledge from Jesus, yet too many times we are actually much more like the audience, who misses the point, and in turn, misses the Kingdom. That is why it is absolutely essential for each of us to read the parables with fresh eyes. We must open our ears to hear the words. We must understand the message Jesus is talking about. And then, we must try to be honest about who we are in the story, no matter where it takes us!

Here is the reality for most of us in the Church. We may have very well read or heard the parables and teachings a thousand times and assume each time that we are the disciples when, in fact, we are the audience who hears the parable but does not understand what it means. We may very well have been claiming that we follow Jesus and may have been saying that we follow His teachings. We may even call or label ourselves Christians, attend a weekly church service, and actively volunteer at our church. But, we have to be comfortable with the idea that, and this may seem provocative or contrary to what you believe as a "saved" person, even though we claim to follow Jesus, and even though we are active and busy in our churches, our eyes and ears may be closed and unable to see or hear the rich message of the Kingdom of God.

A Personal Story

I certainly do not want you to lose hope and throw up your hands in resignation. That is not the intention of this book! It is to *help you* open your eyes and ears to the Kingdom of God. The truth is that your eyes and ears *can always* be opened no matter who you are or where you are at in your own individual journey. It takes an awareness of your current condition and a willingness for the soil of your life to change in order for the Kingdom message to be planted deep so it can take root and grow. Read how Jesus explained this parable of the seed sower to His disciples when He pulled them aside:

> When people hear the message about the Kingdom and do not understand it, the evil one comes and snatches away what was sown in their hearts. This is the seed sown along the path. The seed falling on rocky ground refers to people who hear the word and at once receive it with joy. But since they have no root, they last only a short time. When trouble or persecution comes because of the word, they quickly fall away. The seed falling among the thorns refers to people who hear the word, but the worries of this life and the deceitfulness of wealth choke the word, making it unfruitful. But the seed falling on good soil refers to people who hear the word and understand it. They produce a crop, yielding a hundred, sixty or thirty times what was sown. Matthew 13: 19-23

There are forces at work that can blind us and keep us from seeing, hearing, and realizing the great message of the Kingdom of God. They can also keep this message from taking root and growing in our lives. Though it may be subtle, it is both a reality and a situation to which we must awaken. I have experienced this blindness and deafness firsthand in my own life. The reason I know it is possible to read about Jesus and hear the messages of Jesus, yet still be truly blind and deaf to the message of the Kingdom of God, is that there were forces at work around me that clouded my vision of the Kingdom and kept me from truly hearing its message. I had determined that I had everything figured out. I believed that I was viewing Jesus and the Gospels through the appropriate lens. I believed there was nothing more that I needed to know. It was at that moment when I was caught completely off guard, discovering that I could only see what I wanted to see and only hear what I wanted to hear. As a result, I kept running in circles day after day chasing my own tail.

About ten years ago a friend and I believed that we should start an organization called *Taking Back America*. We believed that the very best thing for America was for Christians to mobilize politically and make a stronger united effort to influence our governments, schools, and other institutions "for the cause of Christ." We were very excited about this endeavor and were planning to have a huge kick-off event with some national political speakers who were Christians and some major label Christian musical acts.

With the planning underway and a few speakers already committed, I contacted a particular artist management company to line up a musician. I spoke to several different people at this company, telling them all about what we were doing and why we were doing it. I sent them our information and they told me that they would get back with me within a couple of weeks, but they never did.

Frustrated, as this was the last piece of the puzzle we needed to begin promoting the event, I called the agency back in order to find out what was taking so long. The lady with whom I had been speaking over the previous weeks finally passed the call over to the agency director. The subsequent conversation left me completely frustrated and confused.

The director started by saying that he did not believe that the musician we were trying to book necessarily agreed with what we were doing or how we were doing it. Perplexed, I asked him to be more specific. He said that neither he nor the musician believed that it was a good thing for Christianity to advance politically, adding that they did not think America necessarily *had* to be "taken back for Christ" by the means we were suggesting.

I continued to press him because I could not understand what he was saying. It was not computing. It would not register. I could not imagine that there could be such a person who did not believe that Christians *ought not* take America back and "restore it to the Christian values and ideals that we once had." Even more frustrated, I asked him how, exactly, we ought to move forward as Christians in America if we do not do it politically.

He told me something I will never forget. He said, "The Kingdom of God is not dependant upon any political or governmental institution to move forward."[12]

That was the first time that anyone who had a very different perspective of the way, life, and message of Jesus had confronted me on my limited perspective of how a Christian should think, act, and behave in our country. Even further, that was the first time anyone had ever mentioned the Kingdom of God to me. It was the first time anyone had ever suggested that God could work and move in the world in ways that were different than anything I had ever known or expected. It certainly got my attention, but I was ANGRY that day. I would have socked that guy in the mouth if we had both been in the same state! How dare this guy challenge my perspective that is *so* obvious and such a good thing for our country! How dare he challenge a viewpoint that is shared by *so many* Christians I know! How dare he think that he knows something that I don't!

Even in my anger, I had to at least admit that my view may have been limited because I had never known or heard anything about the Kingdom of God. I had never heard that the Kingdom of God was a present in-breaking reality in the lives of those who follow the sacrificial way of Christ. Little did I know that I was the one to whom Jesus was referring in His parable. I was the weekly church-attender, the Bible reader, and the one who called myself a Christian (none of which are bad things), but I did not have the eyes to see or the ears to hear and understand the knowledge of the secrets of the Kingdom of God. I was a cultural Christian in every sense of the word who had never been confronted with Jesus and his upside-down Kingdom message. Although my love and desire for the Church were great at that time, my attention was directed toward many of the wrong things and toward many of the wrong pursuits.

Opening our Eyes and Ears

Please don't just easily dismiss what I am saying. You may be the very best person with the greatest intentions for Christ within your church, as I believed I was, but you may have never been confronted with the life-changing and eye-opening reality of the Kingdom of God. You may have never heard about it or even considered it before now. You may have never considered that the cause of Christ in the world could move forward in ways that look very different than the ways you believe it should. You may have never considered how the message and understanding of the

Kingdom of God might change your life, your priorities, your church, and then the world you live in.

For all of your goodness and sincerity, you may think you see, but your eyes may be clouded by cultural lenses that distort reality. Even though you claim to hear, you may not really be able to hear and understand because your hearing is filtered by what you want or think you need to hear. Listen, our hearts can become easily calloused and we may not even know it because we have become religious or gotten caught up in the superficial, dead-end pursuits and pettiness of the Church that have kept the seed of the Kingdom of God from penetrating deep and growing to abundant Life.

Our churches are in desperate need of a new life and a new breath. Our churches are in desperate need of people with open eyes and open ears. Our churches are in desperate need of the Kingdom seed that is sown deep in the rich and welcoming soil of our hearts. Our churches are in desperate need of the life-changing and heart transforming in-breaking Kingdom of God reality. And, our churches are in desperate need for these dead bones in the tombs to come together and resurrect to new life in the power of God. Believe me, when this begins to happen, not only will the Church be transformed, but the world will be changed in power as well.

CHAPTER 3

MODERN DAY PARABLE

I have a garden in my back yard. It isn't big, but we plant a few different types of tomatoes, green beans, and some carrots. I go to sleep each night and wake the next morning to find that the once dormant seeds have come to life. They break through the fertile ground and are drawn to the warm, radiant and welcoming sun, and then are refreshed by the cool waters that fall from the heavens. Who knew that having a garden could be such a spiritual experience?

The crazy thing is that I have several bags of seed in a cabinet in my garage, and not one of the seeds is growing. But see, somehow you already knew that they weren't growing, right? I know this is a ridiculous example, but it doesn't matter who you are, where you live, how much money you make, how intelligent you are, or the time period in which you live, you know intuitively that in order for seeds to grow, they need to be planted in soil that has been worked and cultivated. The seeds must be scattered in the soil by the sower. The water must pour down on the thirsty soil enabling the seed to be nourished. The light must shine down to summon the seedlings to break through the soil and grow. And ultimately, the good fruit will spring forth in bounty from the branches.

Images like this have been understood from the earliest of ages and have cut across cultural, ethnic, educational, economic, and historical lines. That is precisely how Jesus spoke of life's most sacred truths and one of the ways he announced the good news of the Kingdom of God for which He was sent. He used those things that are common to humanity and that could be understood by the Ages. In addition to seeds, soil, birds, and weeds, Jesus used fish, nets, wheat, yeast, dough, workers, employers, and money as visual images to teach people. These are images that people can identify with and that were used in parables to continually reveal the great beauty and mystery of God here on earth for those who have eyes to see and ears to hear and understand. But while, on the one hand, parables may serve as a means to reveal the great beauty and mystery of God to humanity, their messages can, on the other hand, cut people to the core.

One parable that Jesus told to the religious leaders of His day that cut them to the core was about a vineyard. In this parable, the workers ignored the great task in the vineyard that they were given by their boss. Jesus, through His parable teaching, spoke squarely and directly at God's chosen people in Israel who had become incredibly religious, neglecting their identity and task in the world. They were those who had been given the responsibility by the owner of the vineyard, God, the task of producing the fruits of right-living, justice, and mercy for the sake of the world, but they had instead neglected it.

Story of the Vineyard

God is like the owner of a vineyard that stretches along a magnificent hillside. The fruit that God wants to produce in the lives of His people is right-living, justice, and mercy. However, this vineyard, once in its full glory, was devastated by a jealous neighbor, along with his buddies, who was bent on becoming the owner of the vineyard himself. In response, the owner hired some local workers to begin repairing the devastation, with the goal being to build up the vineyard so as to produce a good fruit. The owner of the vineyard entered into a contract, or covenant, with a group of workers who agreed to do the work. They agreed to follow the list prepared by the owner, which would help them repair the devastated vineyard and grow an abundance of fruit.

It was soon apparent that the workers were not repairing and building up the vineyard as they agreed; rather they were further contributing to the devastation and lack of fruit. Israel, the workers whom God hired to work the land and be His image-bearers in the vineyard of the world in order to bring the fruit of right-living, justice, and mercy, became religious, unjust, oppressive, and enslaving to her own people. The vineyard was already in disrepair *before* the workers where hired, but it stayed in state of disrepair *after* they were hired. Because of their negligence, the fruit produced by the workers shriveled and dried up. This angered God, the vineyard owner.

One of Israel's great prophets, Isaiah, described it this way:

> The vineyard belonging to the Lord All-Powerful
> >is the nation of Israel;
> >the garden that he loves
> >is the people of Judah.
> >He looked for justice, but there was only killing.
> >He hoped for right-living, but there were only cries of pain.
> > Isaiah 5:7 NCV

Despite the warnings of the prophet Isaiah, God's people continued to neglect the work. Isaiah wasn't the first, nor was he the last, to speak up against his co-workers on behalf of God, the vineyard owner. The prophets who spoke up on behalf of the owner called on their co-workers, or the people of Israel, to change their ways, understand their identity and responsibilities, and fulfill the agreement they had made to care for the vineyard of the world in order to produce the good fruit of right-living, justice, and mercy. But nothing changed, and the results were always the same. In many instances the workers mistreated, injured, and sometimes even killed those who spoke up about the work that was not being done and the fruit that was not being produced.

The angry vineyard owner, God, hoping for a change of heart from the vineyard workers, finally sent his son to talk to the workers and show them how the work ought to be done. Surely, he thought, they will respect my son. Soon enough the son arrived and began to show the workers, not just through words but through actions, how the vineyard was to be repaired and worked in order to produce the good fruit for which the owner had hoped.

Several of the workers, who were cut to the core because they had let down the vineyard owner, began to follow the son around the garden and help him with the work. The son, Jesus, and the workers who followed him around the vineyard, his disciples, began to repair the broken vineyard lives of the people by sowing the Kingdom seeds in the fertile soil of their hearts. These Kingdom seeds were taking root and growing and producing the good fruit of right-living, justice, and mercy.

This was great news to the vineyard owner, to all of the workers who were following the example of the son, and to everyone the son was inviting to help with the work. The vineyard was being repaired. Seeds were being sown. People from everywhere began to join the good work of repairing the vineyard and scattering the Kingdom seeds to produce good fruit that the owner had hoped for all along.

All of this angered the wretched workers who still refused to join the son in his work. "How dare he come into this place, make us look bad, and take away our workers." Upon hearing the grumbling of the wretched workers, the son met with them and said, "I am taking away the vineyard work from you and am now *giving it to people who will produce good fruit and continue to sow the seeds of the Kingdom of God*. As of this moment, I am also tearing down the wall surrounding this vineyard and opening it wide to people around the world who want to follow my way and extend my Kingdom by producing good fruit of right-living, justice, and mercy, and who will continue to sow the Kingdom seeds throughout the vineyard of the world!" In a rage, the wretched workers tore their clothing, grabbed the son, and began to beat him up. They dragged him up on the hillside for all of the workers in the vineyard to see and then killed him.

Despite their efforts to control the vineyard, the wretched workers were already too late. They were immediately seized and evicted from the premises by the owner. And the vineyard workers, who continued the good work that the son had taught them through his example, were now even more empowered by the way and life of the son than ever. They began announcing that the vineyard was hiring anyone who wanted to follow the example of the son and produce the same good fruit that he had produced. Multitudes of people came from everywhere to work in the newly expanded vineyard of the world. They followed the example of the son diligently to produce good fruit, while continuing to sow the seeds of the Kingdom of God with their hearts, minds, and souls.[13]

The Vineyard

Today, we find ourselves in the same exact vineyard, yet it is not as well maintained as it used to be. We know that there are many factors that can positively or negatively influence the quality of the fruit. As we have found, the most obvious and important factor that can negatively effect the entire vineyard and the quality of the fruit, is if the workers completely neglect the way of the son, ignoring the vineyard and failing to produce good fruit in their lives.

It might seem obvious after reading the previous story, but the vineyard must be tended and cared for appropriately in order to yield a rich bounty of good fruit. Did you get that? If not, let me write that again, but this time more emphatically. It might seem obvious after reading the previous story, *but the vineyard must be tended and cared for appropriately for it to yield a rich bounty of good fruit!* How can the harvest be ready if the workers have neglected the work? If we find ourselves in the same vineyard and it is not being well-maintained or if it is not producing fruit, we, as those who have been given the task of working the vineyard and producing a rich bounty, may have a problem on our hands.

The Vineyard Today

So let's say the vineyard, which stretches along one of the most magnificent hillsides you have ever seen, has been handed over to you and some other workers to fix-up in order to begin producing a good fruit. If you are feeling under-qualified or uneasy about this endeavor at this point, don't worry. Even if you have never worked in a vineyard, the workers you are joining have an intimate knowledge of what it takes to care for this vineyard.

Within the first couple of days on the job you are overwhelmed with excitement. The workers gather together as you begin listening to them talk about the vineyard. You are blown away by their knowledge of the vineyard, the process, and the variety of grapes. Everyday you think, how could people know so much about the process of growing grapes? What a wealth of knowledge! The amount of information you are learning is staggering and invaluable. You have learned so much in such a short amount of time. You are beginning to feel confident and completely prepared to begin the work.

As the days turn into weeks and weeks turn into months, the workers continue to gather together to talk about the same things. They talk about the vineyard, the work, and the grapes. What was once new information has become repetitious, redundant, and really quite religious. Each morning they perform the same routine. They have a group chant that celebrates the graciousness of the owner for letting them gather together. Then, the workers have lunch together. Finally, one of the workers stands in front of the others to speak, and his message is the same each time. He typically talks about how the workers should behave on the job, how the vineyard is falling apart, how the workers need to recruit more potential workers to meet with them, and then wraps it up by saying that he can't wait until the owner calls and invites them to live in his vacation home with him as a bonus for behaving so well on the job.

They usually wrap up the day by discussing their plans for a larger and more up to date maintenance building that will hold more workers, their plans to add more worker programs that will attract and impress more potential workers, and their need for new, clean, and vibrant uniforms so that those who are being interviewed won't think that they have to get dirty on the job. The workers love it! They are just as excited to talk about the run-down vineyard and the vacation home as they were the day before. Long live the vineyard owner!

Quite confused, you begin to wonder if the workers have any intention of really ever going into the vineyard to *do* the work rather than just *talk* about it. What sense does it make to hire more workers and spend more money on facilities and programs when all they do is sit around in the maintenance building all day and talk about how they ought to behave on the job?

Your confusion turns into nervousness as you contemplate whether or not you should confront the workers about the work *they* have neglected. Instead of a prized and abundant vineyard that it could be, and once was becoming, the land has become nothing more than dried and cracked ground, parched and begging for water. The vines and branches are broken, and have been left dangling above the dusty ground. What was expected to be the finest yield of grapes of this age have turned into black, shriveled shells of opportunity lost.

Mustering courage from down deep, you finally gather the workers together and walk them out to the scarred hillside. For what seems like moments of eternity, all you can do is stare at skeleton vines dancing in the dust. Finally, you ask the question that should have been asked a long time ago.

"Fellow workers, look at this hillside! Do you realize that while you have been *talking* about the vineyard, the facilities, the programs, and the vacation home, the work in the vineyard was never done and now it is too late?"

The workers all look at each other in shock and utter amazement as one replies, "What do you mean? We don't understand what you are talking about."

"You don't understand what I am talking about! Are you kidding me? We were hired to work in this vineyard and to produce a good fruit. Not only that, but the owner gave us everything we needed to get the job done and get the job done right! All you have been focusing on is how to be better workers, having bigger and better facilities and programs, and contemplating ways to recruit more workers to hang out with you!"

The workers huddle together as if deliberating a verdict. Finally, the same man who spoke earlier steps forward and announces, "While it is true that we were hired by the owner, you were not correct when you said that we were hired to *do the work*."

"What do you mean!" you yell perplexed and exasperated. "What exactly do you think you were hired for anyway?!"

"Well, *you* may have been hired to *work* in the vineyard, but when *we* were hired all we were asked was, 'Do you *know* how to work a vineyard?' and we said, 'Yes, we most certainly do *know* how to work a vineyard, and we may *know* more about it than any other group of people in the area.' That is how we were hired. We weren't hired to *work* the vineyard. We were hired because we *know* how to work the vineyard. We get together each day to talk about how much we know, and we love it when more workers are hired to learn about all the things we know. That is why we hired *you!*"[14]

The Church and the Vineyard

Much like our story in which the workers talked about their knowledge of the vineyard while working to improve their facilities, programs, and services, the Church has become obsessively inward-focused and more concerned about itself than working in the vineyard of the world. As was noted in the previous chapter, this is one of the central reasons why the Church is viewed as hypocritical and why it has lost credibility with many people throughout the world. The Church talks a good talk, but does not walk the walk. The Church remains untransformed and distant from the great issues in the homes, neighborhoods, and communities of our world.

In the same way it did not make sense for the workers in our story to spend money creating a bigger maintenance building to house more workers who were not working the vineyard, churches spend millions of dollars adding additions and building entirely new facilities to attract new members, while the great vineyard work in our lives and beyond are neglected.

The work that longs to be done begins in our own hearts, minds, and souls through the power of the Holy Spirit in order to produce the abundant fruit of God in our lives, so that we may, in turn, let God work through our lives to sow seeds in the hearts, minds, and souls of others. The vineyard begins in our own hearts and extends outward into the lives of those who are dealing with the great issues of our time: marital struggles, addictions, generational poverty, broken homes, materialism, and so on. The vineyard extends even further into the great global issues of hunger, poverty, and slave and sex trafficking, just to name a few. But while churches are dealing with the affairs of the building, finances, programs and services, petty arguments, self-centered attitudes, judgmentalism, legalism, superficiality, and putting on a good presentation for the consumer, the important matters of right-living, justice, and mercy are being neglected in our lives, our churches, our communities, and throughout the world. There is no doubt that the vineyard is in disrepair. How desperately we need the way of the Son, Jesus Christ!

There is a mind-set that exists with many in the Church who believe the problems of the world ought not to be the concern of the Church. This mentality is much like the workers in our story who said, "We were not hired to *work* the vineyard. We were hired because we *know* how to work the vineyard." Our churches operate as if our *only* function is to "get people saved," have them say the right words, or get them to have the same knowledge about Jesus that "the saved" have. All the while, we run from and neglect the exact task that the "saved" should be compelled to do. Our task as "saved people" is to follow the way and example of Jesus Christ in all aspects of life while taking it into every part of the world, helping others experience liberation and freedom from the entanglements and trappings of the kingdoms of the world. It is not only our task and responsibility to go out into the world and tell others about the way of the Son, Jesus Christ, and to baptize them in His name. We are to also *teach and train* others up in the "life to the fullest" that Christ gives us.[15]

"It is not our job," the church member cries, while complaining that the world is going to hell in a hand-basket. "It is the responsibility of the government, the social service agencies, or other community organizations! The church's responsibility is to 'get people saved and wait for heaven', not to get in the messy affairs of the world." Others cry, "We don't know how God is going to fix all the problems of the world, but I am saved and I know where I am going for eternity." All the while the world stands and watches the mystery and hypocrisy of the self-proclaimed vineyard workers who were hired to work in the vineyard but who live untransformed lives, never leaving the safety of their ever-growing churches and the comfort of their self-serving programs and services, but preaching to the world at arm's length about how it ought to live. Are you hearing me?

If ever there is a parable that needs to be told to our generation, it is this one. The message needs to resonate loud and clear. The workers in the vineyard are being put on alert. You have not been hired solely for the knowledge or information that you have about the vineyard to the detriment of the work that needs to be done. You were hired to live transformed lives and to put your hands to the task. You were hired to be a hand in repairing that which is broken, to work the land, and to produce an abundance of fruit in your own individual lives and in the world around you.

Faith in Action

"But we were saved by grace and not by works!" Great, I agree. That is not the point. Do you not think that your belief, faith, salvation, and knowledge of God transform your individual life *for* the work in the world that God is doing? It is amazing and fantastic that you have a wealth of knowledge about the vineyard and that you enjoy getting together to talk about it, but your knowledge ought to *inform who you are in Christ and your task in the world.* Knowledge, even if it is the right knowledge, without action does not produce fruit. In fact, and as we have seen, knowledge without action does not produce life, but death.

Let me say it another way. Your salvation should not propel you to laziness, self-centeredness, or apathy! *Salvation so affects the entirety of your life that it animates you to progression, not regression or apathy.* Salvation propels your life, your belief, your knowledge toward right-living, justice, and mercy. Salvation breaks outward in your life to an active faith (as if there really is anything other than an *active* faith). The truth of the matter is that faith not lived outwardly is a dead faith. Or, as the New Testament writer James would say, "Faith without works is dead."[16]

We have this puny idea of faith within the Church. It is as if we are absolutely terrified to say that faith is more robust than simply our knowledge about God and individual salvation. We are fearful that if we believe our faith is anything more than just our *knowledge* of God's saving power then someone might think we suddenly believe that our salvation is earned if we put our faith into action. There are movements of Christians who rightly argue that we ought not guilt or coerce Christians to live an outward faith because it is equivalent to a law, and we no longer live under the law. I would point out that Scripture indicates the law has now been written on our hearts through the work of the Holy Spirit. It is through God's law, written on our hearts, that the Spirit makes us alive to live out our faith in real and powerful ways each day.

Faith is so much more than our belief or knowledge about God. Even demons believe and have knowledge of God...and they are demons![17] We certainly do not want to share company with demons by only believing or knowing about God. Faith *has to be more than just something in our heads*. We *live* our faith! Our faith is holistic in the sense that it is the full belief, experience, knowledge, and saving power of God that is so overwhelming and transformative that it changes us at our very core and then expresses itself outwardly in our lives. That is the fullest expression of our faith! One without the other is dead. Faith without action is a dead faith. Action without belief or knowledge in God is a dead faith. The Spirit transforms us to be people used by God in real, everyday life situations. That is faith.

CHAPTER 4

A HOUSE HELD HOSTAGE

What has been missing within the Church for so long is the larger story or narrative in which we find ourselves. We start out as children understanding the stories of the Bible, but we have very little understanding of how the stories necessarily relate to one another, or what function they serve as part of a larger story. We are comfortable looking at and trying to understand them from a 30-foot view, but when we look at them from a 30,000-foot view to see how they all fit together we begin to have problems. We are quick to see and focus only on the individual components of the car, but not the car in its entirety. Of course the individual components of the car are important, but only because they come together to form the larger car.

The message that many of us are left with in our churches is a component of the car. We only preach about the engine of the car week in and week out to the neglect of the entire car. The engine we focus on is, "You are a sinner and need a Savior. Give your life to Jesus so your sins can be forgiven." While the engine is an essential part of the car, no one is telling us about the larger car in which the engine runs.

Please don't think that I do not agree with this statement, because I do with every ounce of my being. I am a sinner in need of a Savior and have been forgiven by the grace of God. *I am not trying to diminish this truth at all.* But the parts of that statement are the components of a much larger car, if you will. The engine is *extraordinarily important* and make the *entire* car run well, but if we only talk about and fixate on one component, like the engine, we will never see or appreciate the larger car.

Reclaiming and Restoring

We have so watered down the message of Christianity that the average person is not aware that there is more going on than the salvation of the individual. If that is all we believe is happening, and if that is all we believe God is interested in, then it is no wonder that we organize and orient our churches to accomplish that one single goal.

What if there is actually more occurring than what we have known or expected? What if there is more to the identity and task of the Christian than what we have actually known and settled for? What if there is a much bigger story unfolding around us that we find ourselves a part of- that yes, includes the salvation of the individual but also includes God reclaiming and restoring the entire created order, otherwise known as *everything*! What if this reclaiming and restoring involves the "saved" people working on behalf of God to be ministers of reconciliation in the world?

If it is true that the Bible is a grand telling of this epic story of God reclaiming and restoring the entire created order through the life, death, and resurrection of Jesus Christ, then how would that change our perspective and our responsibility within the Church of not just being "saved" people, but being transformed and used by God in the task of reclaiming and restoring all things? How would that fundamentally change our lives and priorities as individuals and as churches in how we view the world, our responsibilities, and how we use our time, energy, effort, and resources? What if our perspective suddenly changed from being so self-centered and church-centered to being completely and holistically God-centered in *everything* that we do in our lives?

All of a sudden our interests and priorities may become a lot less about us believing that we are the center of the universe, and more about God and God's reign and God's glory finally taking center stage in every single endeavor and pursuit in which we find ourselves. Imagine that! *It is not about us* but about the wonderful and magnificent riches, glory, and mercies of God in all and through all!

Turning our focus and perspective away from ourselves and toward God is absolutely essential, for when we do we begin to realize that God's purposes and concerns are different than our own. This may be surprising but God loves the entire created order, or everything He magnificently made, of which we are a wonderful and special part. This may be even more surprising but God is working to redeem *all of it*. Sin and death are not the natural order of creation, and as a result *everything* dies. Flowers die. Trees die. Cats die. Dogs die. People die. Stars die. Everything that lives suffers the curse of sin and death, and this is not what God intended from the beginning. God loves his good creation and intends to liberate and restore all of it.

I do not want you to think I am playing fast and loose with the language that I am using. Take a look at one example that you know quite well and that makes my point; it is the verse John 3:16. *For God so love the [kosmos- orderly, harmonious, systematic universe] that he gave his only Son.* The New Testament was written in Greek and the word that was translated as "world" is the Greek word *kosmos*. The word *kosmos* means, "the entire orderly, harmonious, systematic universe," or the entire created order of which God was the creator.

Paul goes even further when he writes about the redemption of not just those who are the sons and daughters of God *but of all creation* in Romans 8:

> For the creation was subjected to futility, not willingly, but because of him who subjected it, in hope that the creation itself will be set free from its bondage to corruption and obtain the freedom of the glory of the children of God. For we know that the whole creation has been groaning together in the pains of childbirth until now. And not only the creation, but we ourselves, who have the first fruits of the Spirit, groan inwardly as we await the redemption of our bodies. Romans 8: 20-23

All of creation groans and longs for liberation and freedom from the curse, just as we do. God has been working throughout human history to liberate and redeem it all, with His great victory culminating in the work and accomplishment of Jesus Christ and the initiation of His Kingdom on earth.

Even the prevailing understanding of the early church was that God was in the process of redeeming and restoring all of creation, but this is not the way we have viewed it or the way we have oriented ourselves in the Church for quite some time. In fact, I can remember at various times being told to replace the word "world" with my name when reading John 3:16. *For God so loved [Brandon] that he gave IIis only Son.* Once again, there is nothing wrong with personalizing it because we are a wonderful and precious part of that which God created and is working to redeem. But, when we personalize our faith to the neglect of God's love for the entire created order and the continuing work of the Holy Spirit that still needs to be done in the world through us, we have made ourselves the only purpose of God's larger plan. This perspective seems quite small and limited. This narrow understanding of individual salvation is exactly what has caused the Church to fixate on the individual components rather than the entire car. Again, *the individual components of the car are absolutely important and do their part to hold the car together quite well, but they are not the entire car.*

The Bible is a written account of God creating that which he called "good," but then that good creation was subjected to the disorder of sin and death and in need of rescue, liberation, and renewal. God did not create something "good" only to give up on it and discard it. In many ways, that would seem like defeat and it would not make much sense. Think about it. Did God create something that He called good, only to toss it aside when it gets hijacked? Of course not! Every single part of it is worth redeeming.

God has been working patiently to take back what is rightfully His by reclaiming it, restoring it, and renewing it. It is within this framework that we find God working through willful, sinful humanity leading up to and culminating in Jesus Christ, the liberator of all creation from the bondage of sin and death, for the creation of a new order, a new humanity, a new Kingdom. But, in order for there to be freedom for His glorious creation, the liberator must defeat the hostile and oppressive forces that lead to death, destruction, and decay.

Invasion

Suppose you have been traveling and have been away from home for quite some time. The anticipation of arriving home continues to grow, as this home is where you find life to the fullest. Your home, which is set alone in some of the most beautifully wooded country imaginable, was built with your own hands and abounds in the wonder and diversity of your handiwork. This is also where you find great delight and joy with your children, some of which are naturally yours with the rest being adopted. While you have been away, your children have been house-sitting and taking care of everything for which you have given them responsibility. Your home is the kind of place that just makes you feel alive and in love with life when you are there with your family.

The landscaping is wonderfully contoured with plants and flowers that awaken the senses. The colors blend together as if to paint a wonderful visual tapestry wrapping around the home. The scents drift upward as a pleasant mixture of heaven and earth. The sounds of a bubbling brook and the gentle singing of the birds and frogs combine in a soothing melody.

The inside of your home is just as magnificent as the outside. Although it is quite simple, each room is perfectly thought out and serves its own individual and unique purpose. All of the woods were hand-selected and crafted into the finest furniture that one could imagine. The art work that comes alive from the walls is the manifestation of your vivid imagination and steady, creative hands. Each room waits to accommodate in its splendor as if an invitation has already been sent to the next guest. All is good and right at home, under the responsible care of your children... so you think.

As you are driving back into town and turn on the last stretch of road leading home you begin to make out a large moving truck parked in the driveway. Your heart begins to beat a little faster while perspiration begins to bead on your forehead. As you get closer, it looks as if someone has broken into your home. You notice that all of your children have been tied up and loaded on the truck with many of your most valuable possessions. To add insult to injury, the criminal has also been destroying everything else in the process. The loading truck was driven destructively through the beautiful landscaping. The windows of your home have been broken, and each piece of art, designed with your inspiration and love, has been tossed out of the broken windows.

These actions speak louder than words. "You no longer have a home here. Your children are being held captive. All of these possessions are now mine." Everything that was good and sacred in this heavenly, peaceful dwelling place has been broken, scarred, and snatched away. All you can do is sit there with a sick feeling in your gut, a knot in your throat, and the accompanying sense that you have been violated in the worst possible way.

It doesn't take long for the feelings of sickness to turn to anger. "Who does this guy think he is anyway?" you say to yourself. "What right does he have to come into my house with a few of his beat-up buddies and hold my children captive? What right do they have to take those things captive that I have put so much time, energy, effort, and love into? To break and tear up such a beautiful, peaceful, and life-giving place? To steal my most valuable possessions and not take care of or appreciate them the way that I do?"

You quickly decide that you can't let this thug and his thug buddies, bent on taking the people and things that you love the most, destroy your most exquisite handiwork and succeed in their hostile and devious plan. After sizing up the situation and the thieves, you decide that with a well thought out plan you can overpower the ringleader and tie him up. While he looks like a strong man, you know that you are stronger. By your calculations the other henchmen won't put up much resistance and may very well just run off once the leader is tied up and your children released.

It is finally time to make your move. Slowly you begin to walk along the edge of the woods where you can get a better vantage point looking in through the large window in the back of your house. You wait for just the right moment when the henchmen are all outside next to the moving truck and the ringleader is still inside, and then you make your move. In a full sprint you break through the back door, tackle the ringleader, and easily subdue and tie him up. In the commotion, and as you run out the front door, the other henchmen see what is happening and take off running into the woods.

As you get in the loading truck to untie your emotionally distraught children, you tell them that they are all safe and that the ringleader has been subdued and tied up. Together, you and your children walk back into the tattered house to assess the damage.

As you make your way through your home, you notice that your children are comforting each other and beginning to pick up what has been broken and strewn about in order to put it back together for you. Before long, your children have completely taken over the once broken and violated house. They are following your example by cleaning and straightening up each room, repairing everything that was broken, and putting your handiwork back in order.

In every room that you begin to gather up what has been thrown about and broken, your children also race into and help with the work. You are so proud and appreciative as you realize how blessed you are to have such an amazing family that is helping you reclaim and restore your good home, and help you put all of the pieces back together. Once you are certain that your house is in good hands and are confident that your children have everything they need to get the place back in order, you return to your travels and promise that you will return very soon. The children, anticipating your return and wanting everything in order when your return, work diligently to get your home back in order.[18]

Creation Held Captive

Within this parable we find the larger story that we have been missing for so long. We find the framework for unpacking the great news of the Kingdom of God that Jesus came to announce. There is the home that was creatively crafted in love to bless all who live there, which is God's good and beautiful creation in which we live. There is the thief who was bent on breaking into the home, holding the owner's family captive, stealing the owner's most valuable possessions, and destroying all of the owner's good work, which is Satan and the forces that work to oppose and destroy God's good creation. There is the owner of the home, which is Jesus (but was you for the sake of our story), who poured life, imagination, skill, and talent into the design and craftsmanship of the home and then later broke into the home to bind up the thief and release the children who were being held captive. There are the natural and adopted children, the children who follow the way of Jesus, who were all held captive by the thief and then who later helped their father reclaim the home, gather up that which was taken, and repair and restore the home when the father went away so he could return with everything in order.

The world is like a house that Satan and the powers of evil broke into, took captive, and are bent on destroying. Jesus is the father who broke into the house in order to tie up the Adversary and release His children, the people of the world who follow His way. This is the way Jesus described the state of affairs in our world. He came to break into the kingdom of the world, tie up the adversary, and free His children to continue on the restorative work in the world through the power given to them by the Holy Spirit.

Jesus understood creation as God's beautiful and creative handiwork made in love, but also as a creation being held captive, ravaged in the present evil age by the powers and principalities who oppose the glory of God. Jesus told the story this way:

For when a strong man like Satan is fully armed and guards his palace, his possessions are safe- until someone even stronger attacks and overpowers him, strips him of his weapons, and carries off his belongings. Anyone who isn't with me opposes me, and anyone who isn't working with me is actually working against me. Luke 11: 21-23 NLT

From the perspective of Jesus, there is a strong man guarding a house and this strong man must be dealt with. The strong man has taken control of a place which is not rightly his but that he now calls his own. He has claimed *everything* in the house as his own property. He has even taken the most beloved possessions captive, the children.

With this understanding there is a sense of injustice and enslavement that must be dealt with and made right. Again, there is something that has been unjustly taken that must be reclaimed, not just the children but the whole house. The home has been broken into and is in need of an eviction. The children being held hostage are in need of a liberator, a savior. But we are moving ahead too quickly, and it is enough to say for now that an occupying force has broken into the house, is holding it captive, and is bent on destroying it in the process.

Common Thread

The early biblical writers understood that all of God's beautiful creation, which God declared as "good" from the very beginning, has been subjected to "hostile, proud, raging, destructive forces of chaos [that] oppose God's will and threaten the very foundations of the earth."[19] They refer to an *opposing force* as the Hebrew word *ha satan*, which simply means "the adversary" or "the accuser." *Ha satan* refers to *any* adversary or opponent in *any* situation. But in certain specific instances in the Old Testament, it refers to an angelic being that is at work to oppose and disrupt the glory of God's good creation. It is an oppositional force that works toward the breaking and fragmenting of individual people, relationships between people, and the relationship between people and God.

In other words, God's beautiful and magnificent creation, which was once whole, complete, and full of the *shalom* (or peace) of God, has been hijacked, fragmented, and turned into a battle field that is in dire need of rescue and restoration. This is certainly not to say that humanity does not have free-will in how and what we choose, but it is to say that this is the situation in which we find ourselves- the "tragic intrusion [of evil] into God's otherwise good creation."

New Testament writers echo the same sentiment in their understanding of the present evil age and the occupying evil force who enslaves and oppresses humanity and the rest of God's good creation. John writes in one of his letters that the entire created order, or *kosmos*, is "under the control of the evil one."[20] He continues on in the apocalyptic of Revelation:

And there was war in heaven. Michael and his angels fought against the dragon, and the dragon and his angels fought back. But he was not strong enough, and they lost their place in heaven. The great dragon was hurled down—that ancient serpent called the devil, or Satan, who leads the whole world astray. He was hurled to the earth, and his angels with him. Revelation 12: 7-9

And:

The heavens and those who dwell in them should rejoice and those on earth and the sea should be filled with grief and distress because the adversary, Satan, and other adversarial angels have gone down to you! He is filled with fury, because he knows that his time is short. Revelation 12: 12

Paul describes the adversary as the "prince of the power of the air" who works *in those who are in opposition to God*.[21] Paul is clear, however, when he declares that this war we find ourselves in is not against flesh and blood or human beings but against the rulers, authorities, and powers of this dark world and the spiritual forces in the heavenly realm. Powerful, antagonistic forces are at work to divide, crush, and conquer God's good creation and use broken humanity in the process for their destruction. It is worth remembering the words of Jesus from the parable of the Strong Man, "Anyone who isn't with me opposes me, and anyone who isn't working with me is actually working against me."

There is a great cosmic war raging that plays out on the stage of human history, and humanity is a means through which the reign of Satan can break into existence into our lives and into our affairs if we allow it. Again, it is important for us to recognize that our battle is not against humanity itself but against the adversarial forces that work to enslave, oppress, and reign on earth *through* humanity. This point is critical, and it's one we have not learned so well in the Church.

Paul continues on in another letter writing that the adversary, Satan, is "the god of this age" that blinds the minds of the unbelieving so they may not see the light of the good news of the Kingdom of God.[22] In essence, there are spiritual forces at work in the world *who have blinded the minds of unbelievers and have the power to influence and affect the powers and authorities of this world who work in opposition to the reign and rule of God.*

If Satan and the other adversarial forces have enslaved and disrupted all of God's good creation, have influenced and affected the powers and authorities of this world in order to thwart the reign of God on earth, and have blinded the minds of the unbelieving from seeing the light of the Good News of the Kingdom of God, then we have no other choice than to conclude that this is not what God has intended for his good creation. A strong man broke into a house that was not his own, took it captive, and has worked to divide and conquer it. In order to reclaim the house, someone more powerful must break in, tie up the strong man, and liberate the house.

In this, we may have gotten a first glimpse of the good news that Jesus came to announce in the story of the strong man. *In Jesus a covert operation was initiated to break in to the house, tie up the strong man, and then, along with his children, reclaim what is rightfully God's, renewing and restoring that which has been broken. In Jesus, one kingdom was broken into and overthrown in order to reestablish the Kingdom of God. The subjects of this Kingdom of God give their full allegiance to Lord Jesus and operate by the holy and righteous standards of God through the power of the Holy Spirit.*

The Problem

You can see the problem that we have in front of us. On the one hand the Church has been compromised by those who have found other more valuable "riches and treasures" that they would like the world to come and see and have buried the great treasure of the Good News of the Kingdom of God that Jesus came to announce and establish. On the other hand, we have adversarial forces at work to keep the entire created order enslaved. These forces are at work to establish and advance the reign of Satan on earth while blinding the minds of the unbelieving so they might not see and perceive or hear and understand the Good News of the Kingdom of God and how it would liberate them from their slavery. In essence, the Church has stopped announcing and living it, and the world is enslaved, blinded, and unable to hear it or see it. What a dilemma.

This is incredibly important and revealing for the purposes of the Church. If the Good News of the Kingdom of God has been buried, it must be rediscovered and unearthed by people who are tirelessly looking for it and then tirelessly announcing it and living it out, praying that God would open the eyes, ears, and hearts of the entire world that is enslaved by the forces of evil. We must fight with prayer and fasting against the powers and principalities of evil that keep people from seeing and perceiving and from hearing and understanding so that they may be brought into the freedom of the Kingdom of God. We, as the Church, must be instrumental in working toward liberating the captives by taking the light of Christ and the Good News of His alternative Kingdom into every dark area of people's lives and into every dark corner of the world. The world does not need more religion; it needs a rescue from the enslaving and victimizing kingdoms of the world. The only alternative to the kingdom of the world is the Kingdom of God. But who is announcing and living out this Kingdom?

It Starts With Us

The Church, by living out the Kingdom of God in our lives, *must* be the alternative to the kingdoms of the world. *We* have to be the people with our eyes and ears opened wide to the realities of this house that is being held hostage and the desperate need of a saving and life-giving Kingdom. Otherwise, we just continue as the blind leading the blind.

If there is Good News that Jesus announced and that the enslaved world needs to hear but they have not heard because we have not known about it ourselves, then we must rediscover it for the sake of the world so that the riches, glory, and mercies of God can be once and for all revealed, clearly seen, and experienced by all. We must rediscover the Kingdom of God and go on the spiritual offensive rather than sitting idly by and watching the world get ravaged and torn apart by the oppressive forces of evil. We must rediscover the Kingdom of God so that the reign of Satan will be put on the defensive and then rightly overthrown and replaced by the reign of God here on earth and throughout the entire cosmos. So while we wait patiently for the return of our Lord and the fullness of His Kingdom to be ushered in, let us live presently as citizens of this Kingdom, as citizens of heaven, and in a manner worthy to be called the sons and daughters of God for the sake of an enslaved world.

Is there anything more essential for the Christian right now than to go back to the words, teachings, and life of Jesus to understand exactly what He believed his mission to be, to uncover how He announced it to the world, and to [re]discover the Kingdom to which He is calling His followers to? Is there any cause more important than those who have been blinded to the Kingdom of God to receive sight and those who have been deaf to the Kingdom of God to now hear the Kingdom reality announced by Jesus? Isn't it more important now than ever that we, as Christians, cast aside our preconceived notions of what we think we believe, and discard those things we have created that keep us from being the means through which the Kingdom of God breaks into the world in power?   Should we not be ready and willing to toss aside empty traditions, rules, protocols, and power that continue to consume us and divide us in order that we be united and a testament to the world that the Lord is One? Is there any better time than now to put your own self-interest and preferences aside and break free from hollow, empty religion or from an artificial and superficial church? Is there any better time than now to make Jesus Christ and His Kingdom the centerpiece of our identity and purpose in the world?

Let us open our eyes and our ears to the Kingdom announcement of Jesus. Become a searcher and discoverer of His Truth. Join the united movement of those who are asking, seeking, and knocking so that the door will be opened unto us. For it is in this asking, seeking, and knocking that we will once and for all discover, be amazed, and become the fullness of the Body of Christ in and for the enslaved world.

CHAPTER 5

THE YEAR OF THE LORD'S FAVOR

Can you imagine running into your house, grabbing the thief, and then right before you get ready to tie him up he says, "I'll tell ya what, here's the deal. Even though I broke into your house and am having my way with it, I will let you have your house back. But there is a catch. I will run this house my way and you will have to serve me and operate by my rules."

Tweaking our previous story a little, I am sure that we all can quickly agree that a scenario like that is just insane. It doesn't make any sense. In fact, it is completely counter-intuitive to everything that we think and know. Why would *your* home now belong to a thug who just recently broke in, ransacked the place, and took your family captive? How ridiculous and audacious would it be for the thug to offer to let you and your family still live there? Even more, how unbelievable would it be for the thug to have the nerve to suggest that *you and your children need to serve him and operate by his rules*! The house is still your house. Your children are still your children. The best thing that could happen is for you to tie up the thief, set your children free, and get your home back in order.

Confrontation

If that story sounds familiar at all, it should. In a dramatic confrontation right before Jesus began his public ministry, the adversary approached Jesus at the end of his forty-day fast and tempted him.[23] In one of the more peculiar, and in our case insightful exchanges, Satan led Jesus to a very

49

high place and showed him *all the kingdoms of the world.* And to Jesus he said, "I will give you all their authority and splendor, for it has been given to me, and I can give it to anyone I please. So if you worship me, it will all be yours." In other words, "If you serve me and follow my rules, I will let you have your house back."

I am sure that if you are like me you would have a few things to say to a trespasser, thief, kidnapper, and ransacker. I can think of a few *hundred* things that I might say, and some of them aren't very nice! But Jesus calmly responds, "It is written: 'Worship the Lord your God and serve him only.'" It is as if Jesus, with such a short and simple response, knows something that the adversary doesn't know. It is almost like He is thinking, "You are already defeated and you don't even know it. You have been operating on borrowed time. I'm about ready to tie you up, turn this world upside down, release the prisoners and captives, and put this thing back in order, and you have no idea what is coming. I am like the Trojan horse breaking into enemy-occupied territory and unleashing the most subversive counter-attack in the history of the world against you!" Don't you love it?

Jesus doesn't spend time arguing with him, *which may be a great lesson for all of us,* about whose house it really is or who was there first. He simply replies, "Worship God and serve Him only." And it is with that one statement that the proverbial "line in the sand" was drawn. Either we worship you or we worship God. Either we serve you or we serve God. It is either your way or God's way. We can either be citizens in your kingdom or in God's Kingdom. There's no straddlin', no half-steppin', and no dual allegiance in this place. We can't have one foot in one kingdom and another foot in the other Kingdom. The battle line has been drawn and it is now time to choose sides. In Jesus, the rescue operation was initiated. The enslaved created order that had been broken into and held hostage was being reclaimed and set free. The reign of Satan was being confronted by the Reign of God. The kingdoms of the world were being overthrown by the Kingdom of God. The whole working order of the world was about to be turned completely upside down.

Announcement

But how do you notify those around you that you are the long awaited Messiah, the Anointed One who is about to turn the ways and workings of the world upside-down? I am just curious. How do you announce that you have been sent to set the captives free and to make the blind see, anyway?

If you are going to make a big announcement like that, you may want to do it in the biggest way possible, you know, on a big day with a lot of important people around. At least that is my thinking.

Making a big announcement usually sends people buzzing and talking about it for quite some time. News cycles run big announcements over and over and over until they are sure they have covered every possible angle of the story. People talk about and debate big announcements at the water cooler at work and at the local pubs. In the United States we go into an absolute frenzy when a person simply announces his or her intention to run for president! So you can imagine a Jewish man taking center stage in a Jewish synagogue, sitting in front of the respected Jewish religious leaders of the day, asking for a scroll and reading:

> The Spirit of the Lord is on me,
> because he has anointed me
>> to preach good news to the poor.
>> He has sent me to proclaim freedom for the prisoners
>> and recovery of sight for the blind,
>> to release the oppressed,
>> to proclaim the year of the Lord's favor.

> The Scripture you've just heard has been fulfilled this very day.

> Luke 4: 18-19, 21

If you had been sitting in the audience that day, as a good Jew, you would have understood the reading of those words much differently than you do now. As a Jew hearing that proclamation, you would have had a deep sense of expectation and excitement that Yahweh (God) was finally acting in history to liberate and vindicate your people, God's holy and chosen people, against the foreign pagan oppressors and the idolatry that had been enslaving your people for so long.

No doubt you would have been sitting in the audience thinking about the faithfulness of Yahweh and everything that your ancestors had been through and what you and your family were currently going through. It had been a long and difficult journey, but could it be that Yahweh was finally sending the long-awaited Messiah to make things right and to bring justice? Could it be that Yahweh was finally sending His Messiah to crush the foreign enemies that had been heavy-handed toward your people? Could it be that Yahweh was finally acting decisively in history to rescue your people from their idolatrous ways so as to be their first and only love?

The announcement of Jesus would have sent your mind reeling, thinking back about Yahweh's restoration plan through one faithful man, Abraham, and his family, who God said would outnumber the stars. You are a part of this family who was to be a blessing to all nations by being the image-bearers of God in the world. You are a part of a family who was given the task of putting the broken pieces of the world back together so as to restore the shalom (peace) of God among the nations and throughout the world. But your mind quickly shifts to think about how your people, the people of the promise, have suffered greatly at the hands of those who made God their enemy.

How terrible it was for our ancestors to be enslaved by the Egyptians, you think. But you also remember how Yahweh was faithful. Working through His servant Moses, Yahweh delivered the Israelites out of slavery, through the water, and into freedom. And it was in that freedom that your people, the Israelites, received the law of God. It was the law given to your people to mold them and craft them into the likeness of Yahweh, in order to live out and extend the righteousness, justice, and mercy of God to the world.

Your mind quickly shifts to thinking about how many ups and downs your people had experienced in their faithfulness to God, who you refer to as Yahweh. The Israelites wanted a king like the other nations instead of Yahweh being their only King. Despite a rocky start and their first king not working out so well, the great Golden Age in Israel was at its height during the reign of their second king, David. All was good and right in the Kingdom of God under the kingship of David. The nation was strong, rich, and at peace.

If it wasn't the ups and downs of your people continually turning from Yahweh, compromising righteousness and their holy identity while putting their trust in pagan idols, it was the continual enslavement to the foreign pagan oppressors. The Golden Age in Israel was a distant memory, and you could almost hear the haunting cries of your ancestors, "Yahweh, if we are your holy, chosen people who are to be a light among the nations then why are we continually enslaved and oppressed?" It was the recurring cry of a people under the weight of kingdom after kingdom: the Egyptians, the Assyrians, the Persians, the Babylonians, the Greeks, and the Romans. The nation of Israel had been invaded, held captive, dispersed throughout many lands, and then returned to their land only to be under the weight of a new occupying force. The peace and prosperity that was once experienced for a short amount of time in their past was now a distant memory.

The past you know so well through the reading of Torah, the first five books of the Old Testament, and the retelling of its stories does not seem so distant now. The ancient cries of your ancestors are the present cries of you and your people who are now under the tight fist of the Roman Empire, and this empire is one of the most ruthless in history. Not only are the roads lined with dead bodies on crucifixes to remind you that Rome is in control, but nearly all of your income is taken from you in the form of tithe, tax, and tribute, leaving you and others frustratingly poor. You feel helplessly oppressed and enslaved. You hardly feel chosen. Maybe more like forgotten.

"Has Yahweh forgotten us? Will Yahweh ever give us a deliverer like Moses who will lead us out of captivity and into freedom once and for all? Will Yahweh again give us a king like King David who will once and for all defeat the pagan oppressors and restore the Kingdom of God? Will Yahweh ever send the Anointed One who has been spoken of through the prophets so long ago?"

All of these thoughts come together as you hear this Jesus, who had been spoken of as the Anointed One since his birth, announcing now that he is indeed the Anointed One. He is the one who will proclaim freedom to the enslaved and oppressed. He is the one who will lead the captives out from under the weight and strain of bondage. He is the one who will announce that there is good news for the poor. And, he is the one who is announcing the Year of the Lord's favor.

There was certainly a buzz of excitement along with some cynicism and skepticism that day. Some people argued that Jesus was just another in a long line of freedom fighters who called themselves Messiahs and who tried to rally the troops against the mighty Roman Empire, only to be crushed and put on display for the people see. Others were not so dismissive, especially when Jesus read that he was announcing the Year of the Lord's favor. That was something to get really excited about!

The Year of the Lord's Favor

Everyone knew that the Year of the Lord's favor referred to the Year of Jubilee. Within the law that God gave Moses and the Israelites was instruction to celebrate the Sabbath year. This meant that every seventh year the land, animals, and people were to be given a rest from work. It was a time for rejuvenation. During the Sabbath year, Yahweh would care for the people and provide everything they needed. After seven cycles of seven Sabbaths (forty-nine years) the people would then celebrate the 50th year as a Jubilee year, or the Year of the Lord's favor.[24]

Like a Sabbath year, the land, animals, and people would be given rest from work during the Jubilee year. But what made the Jubilee year special was Yahweh's instruction to the people to proclaim freedom throughout the land. All lands would be returned to their original owners. All debts incurred would be cancelled. The poor would no longer be oppressed or taken advantage of. The slaves would be made free. The Year of the Lord's favor was a great reminder that since Yahweh brought the Israelites out of slavery and into freedom, they should continue the blessing by freeing the oppressed and enslaved brother or sister in their land.

That is why so many people were excited when they heard the announcement of the Year of the Lord's Favor in Jesus' reading. Could it be that the time of judgment, freedom, and vindication had finally come? Could Jesus be like Moses and lead God's people out of slavery and bondage and into freedom once and for all? Could Jesus be like the great King David who had finally come to vindicate Israel from the foreign pagan oppressors and usher in another Golden Age in the Kingdom of God? Could Jesus be the one who would reclaim the land, cancel the debts, let the slaves go free, and proclaim the Year of the Lord's favor? The excitement was certainly building.

Little did they know that the announcement of Jesus was bigger than anything they could even get their head around. Little did they know that Jesus wasn't just coming like another Moses only to free the enslaved Israelites. He was coming to lead humanity out of slavery to sin through the waters of baptism and into the glorious freedom of God. Little did they know that Jesus wasn't coming only to proclaim the good news of the Kingdom to the poor of Israel but to proclaim the Good News of the Kingdom to every person in the world. Little did they know that Jesus wasn't coming only to reclaim the land of Israel that had been occupied by governmental forces but coming to reclaim the entire created order that had been occupied by the oppositional forces of evil. Little did they know that Jesus just wasn't coming only to cancel the debts of the poor in Israel but of every single sinful person who was indebted to God. Little did they know that Jesus wasn't coming just as another King David to vindicate Israel, defeat the pagan oppressors, and restore a bricks and mortar political kingdom but that he was coming to break into the kingdoms of the world, draw a line in the sand, vindicate humanity, and defeat the Adversary and the powers and principalities of evil in order to establish a new Kingdom in the hearts and minds of those who follow Him and who call Him Lord.

That is how you make an announcement full of power! An announcement with that much history and full of that much anticipation certainly got everyone's attention. Jesus wasn't interested in all talk and no show. He was interested in proclaiming the Kingdom of God *and* demonstrating the Kingdom of God. He was interested in teaching and training his disciples, not just with His words, but with His life. So much more than anyone had expected was at stake, and God was acting decisively and unexpectedly in history through Jesus Christ to proclaim the Year of the Lord's Favor for all of creation, especially humanity.

The Kingdom of God was launched and established in the hearts and minds of those who believe. The blind would now see. The enslaved would now be free. The poor would now be made rich. The tables of history would now be turned upside down. The rogue kingdoms of the world would finally and decisively suffer defeat. The Kingdom of God was on the march. It was not a matter of talk, but of power. And in Jesus Christ was the life and power to overthrow the adversarial forces of evil, defeat sin and death, release captive humanity, reclaim that which is rightfully God's, and initiate His Kingdom reign on earth as it is in heaven!

CHAPTER 6

SPREADING WILDLY AND OUT OF CONTROL

It spreads like an infection or a virus. The smallest part can work its way through the entire system. It doesn't happen by simple addition. It multiplies and multiplies and multiplies until it has fully, and finally, taken over. It is an invasion of something that breaks in from the outside and then completely takes over.

It may even be understood as a small seed that turns into an invasive plant. All it takes is for the seed to take root and then it grows into a large plant that is wild, spreading out of control. It starts off insignificant and unassuming, but then becomes extraordinarily invasive, taking over everything in its path. It towers upward and then spreads outward, growing profusely, replicating, and preventing anything else around it from taking root.[25]

Some may even understand it as yeast that is put into a batch of dough. All it takes is for the single-cell of yeast to be put in a moist environment and fed some sugar for it to begin multiplying rapidly. It doesn't take long for this small amount of yeast to multiply and spread until it is completely worked through the dough.[26]

These images capture the essence of the Kingdom of God. The Kingdom of God is an invasion. It is an infection. It is one small part breaking into the larger system, disrupting it, and taking it over. It is that which is with-out, breaking with-in our time/space reality and progressively and completely transforming it. It is heaven breaking into the created order and destroying the works of Satan until heaven and earth are finally joined together as one at the coming together, the consummation of all things through Jesus Christ.

The Kingdom of God comes to life in Jesus. It is Jesus breaking into the kingdoms of the world, disrupting them by embodying the Kingdom of God with His life, death, and resurrection so His followers, who look and act like Him in everything they do, can continue to spread this Kingdom infection through their words and actions. The sole purpose of this invasive and offensive action by Jesus is to displace the ways, workings, and conventions of the kingdoms of the world with the Kingdom of God. It is God's plan through Jesus Christ and the working of His Spirit to renew, heal, mend, and restore that which is fractured and broken by the devastation of sin. It is an offensive action to turn the kingdoms of the world completely upside-down, turning hate to love, violence to peace, injustice to justice, weeping to joy, fear to faith, and self-centeredness to selfless sacrifice.

The invasion of the Kingdom of God in Jesus is a full-on assault and overthrow of Satan and the powers and principalities of evil in this world, so as to establish the Reign of God throughout the entire created order. This Kingdom invasion is a complete toppling and overthrow of a rogue, fly-by-night kingdom that has worn out its welcome. It is a new reality that has broken into the tired, old, worn-out, predictable ways of the world and is replacing them with a new and higher way that offers love, healing, hope, and life to the fullest.

Quite literally, it is heaven breaking into every dimension of our world like an infection, like an invasive plant that is taking over and growing wildly, like yeast that is multiplying and multiplying and multiplying until it has worked its way through the entire batch. It is the in-breaking and uniting of that which had been separated and fragmented. It is the great marriage, the great uniting, the great consummation of the two, heaven and earth becoming one...even in you.

Sheep Pens

Even further, the Kingdom of God can be understood as a shepherd who brings together his flock in a pasture and constructs an ancient sheep-pen made of large rocks that encircle the entire flock of sheep. When it is time to let the sheep out of the pen, the shepherd removes a few rocks and passes through the opening before the sheep. The sheep then begin rushing through the opening, violently breaking out of the pen through the small open space, anticipating freedom. They cannot escape from the sheep pen fast enough. The sheep break forth out of the small opening running into the freedom that the Shepherd has given them. The Shepherd creates a breach for the sheep and the sheep break out with great force and power. That is what the Kingdom of God is like. The follower of Jesus is like a sheep that breaks through the barriers and limitations of the kingdoms of the world, and runs forcefully behind the way of Jesus the Shepherd, advancing the Kingdom of God.[27]

A follower of Jesus is an invader of every nook and cranny, every pocket, every square inch of hell on earth, taking it over and reclaiming it for heaven and taking back what is rightfully God's. And this invasion reminds us of the most simple prayer of Jesus, "Your Kingdom come, your will be done, on earth as it is in heaven." Yes, on earth as it is in heaven. Let the two become one. Let us be the means through which heaven begins its invasion of the kingdoms of the world.

Offensive Action

The Kingdom of God is an invasion, a securing, and a reclaiming. It is not a defensive stance, but an offensive movement. It is not a group of people sitting around behind the walls of a church cowering in fear that the world is going to hell-in-a-hand-basket. It is not a bunch of people doubting or second-guessing what they ought to be doing in the world or worrying about what other people think of their Kingdom lives. It is not a group of religious people sitting around a table voting whether or not God is in something or not, trying to determine if it makes logical or financial sense, or trying to hype something up for the amusement of their church. It is not a group of people satisfied with showing up at church on Sunday and then checking it off the list.

We do not realize the power of God that works through each of us as His people to destroy the works of Satan and extend His Kingdom. If I asked you how Satan and the powers and principalities are defeated, you would quickly answer by saying, "By the blood of Jesus Christ through His death and the power of His resurrection." If I suggested that there was more to it than that, you may call me a heretic. But look at what John writes in the twelfth chapter of Revelation:

Now have come the salvation and the Kingdom of our God, and the authority of His Christ. For the accuser of our brothers, who accuses them before our God day and night, has been hurled down. They overcame him by the blood of the Lamb *and by the word of their testimony.* Revelation 12: 11

Can you imagine that! We join in on the offensive march against the Adversary and the oppressive forces of evil. Our testimonies of how Jesus Christ brought us out of slavery and captivity and into the glorious freedom of His Kingdom defeats the Accuser and brings more people out of the kingdoms of the world and into His Kingdom. We are a group of people who have mobilized behind Jesus the Liberator, embodying and advancing the freedom of the Kingdom of God. We are those who are transformed by the redemptive work of God through Jesus Christ and the power of the Holy Spirit, and then who break out of captivity in power, invading the entire house and ransacking the kingdoms of the world for heaven. The gates of hell will not stand because these Kingdom people are on the offensive march and are bent on breaking down every stronghold and reclaiming what is rightfully God's through our words, our lives, and our all.[28]

Sent for the Kingdom

The preaching and living out of the Kingdom of God was the purpose for which Jesus was sent. He said it himself. As he was traveling throughout Galilee healing people and driving out the many demons that were afflicting, enslaving, and oppressing the people, the crowds continued to follow him. But when he began to leave for another town, the crowds protested his leaving. To this Jesus responded, "I must preach the Good News of the Kingdom of God to the other towns also, because *that is why I was sent.*"[29]

The purpose for which Jesus was sent into the world was to preach and live out the Kingdom of God! To announce that the invasion has been initiated and it looks like His way and His life in everything we do! To announce that the greatest revolt in history is underway and those who join the revolution look like their leader in every single thought, action, and deed. To announce that God's Kingdom has broken into the kingdoms of the world and it is overthrowing and replacing them with a new and higher way. To announce that the powers and principalities of evil have been defeated and the Reign of God has been initiated. To announce that the blind will finally see, the enslaved will be free, the debt will be paid, and the land will be reclaimed. To announce that all who have faith in Him will be empowered to extend the Kingdom of God throughout the world. To announce that the so-called wisdom and ways of the kingdoms of the world have been turned completely upside-down and replaced with the wisdom and ways of God. And this Kingdom is not just staying in one place. It is on the move. It is on the march. It is growing. It is spreading. It is infecting every person in every city and town around the world, and there is not one person, one group of people, or any one government or institution that can stop it! And we are the means through which God is extending it in the world! Praise God!

A Revolution

I am going to step on *all of our* toes here, including mine, but each one of us in the Church must understand that Jesus was not sent to create a cute little religion. He wasn't sent to establish a group of "holier than thou" or self-righteous people. He wasn't sent to start a country club with benefits for every member. He wasn't sent to originate a fluffy, feel-good, superficial entertainment center that has to feed the world with sweet sugar puffs. He wasn't sent for a group of people who say that they love Him but spend their time being lazy, apathetic, self-focused, and superficial. He wasn't sent so that the religious argue, bicker, and divide over the *exact* interpretation of Scripture. He wasn't even sent so ministers could preach four-point sermons and give quick, easy answers that a bunch of people simply fill in the blanks on Sunday. All of that cheapens and waters down the central purpose of Jesus.

Jesus was sent to announce the greatest revolution in the history of the world and we have been invited to continue the revolution by following the charge of the leader! The people who are joining this revolution, who are spreading the infection, look, act, and behave like the one who is leading the charge.

Gone are the days of simply saying, "Yeah, well that is Jesus and we are not Jesus so we can't be expected to live like him." That is a lie straight from the pit of hell that we have believed for far too long. Yes, we are sinners saved by the grace of God, but we have been brought from slavery and into freedom by Jesus who paid the highest cost for it. We have been renewed, transformed, and empowered by the *very* Holy Spirit of God to be the *very*

Body of Jesus in the world today! The same God that created our entire existence from nothing and moves in the most mighty and miraculous ways ever known to mankind has given unspectacular YOU His power! We have been given the fresh breath of the Spirit and have been made into the new creation people who take up our crosses daily to follow the way of Christ in order to bring heaven on earth![30]

We are the infected...spreading the Kingdom infection throughout the entire body of the world. We are the mustard seeds planted in the garden that are taking over the entire garden. We are the yeast working our way through the entire batch of dough...multiplying and expanding. So put away your cheap excuses, your tired arguments, and your helpless attitudes and join the KINGDOM REVOLUTION of those who are becoming the Body of Christ in the world today, destroying the works of Satan and bringing the Reign of God here and now in great anticipation of the fullness of the Kingdom of God at Christ's return! And the Spirit cries out, "Rise, rise Body! Awaken from your sleep! Rise from the dead and come to Life!"

CHAPTER 7

UNEARTHING THE KINGDOM OF GOD

Revolution, offensive, breaking out with force, taking over, and battling the forces of evil. These words and phrases are so super-charged that they could be easily taken the wrong way by a variety of people, even those who are good and well-intentioned. As I discussed before, depending on the influences and biases that a person has or the lens through which a person views the world, it is possible for two people to view the same exact situation or scenario in a variety of ways.

One person could very easily read the words and teachings of Jesus and understand correctly that the best and highest way for the Kingdom of God to move forward is through a humble and submissive love that lays its life down for friend and enemy alike. Another could *selectively* read the words and teachings of Jesus and again, depending on the lens through which that person views the world, may believe that the best way for the Kingdom of God to move forward is through governments, politics, and maybe even force or violence.

Unfortunately we have seen this kind of gross misinterpretation throughout history and the damage it has done for the cause of Christ in the world. Groups of people have mobilized, supposedly in the name of Jesus, ready to take the Kingdom of God to the nations by physical force, or by making it the national religion, or by politicizing it among the populace, while completely missing the point of the Good News of the Kingdom of God. Again, the Kingdom that Jesus preached and lived out through His life was that of humility and a love that lays its life down for friend and enemy alike. The Kingdom of God can only move forward when it looks exactly like Jesus Christ.

Political Kingdom?

Even the people sitting on a hillside two-thousand years ago listening to Jesus initially thought he was rallying the troops for a physical and violent revolution. In fact, they very well may have thought they were joining the greatest military and political revolution in history! One can only imagine what it was like to be in the crowd that day. The pressure and tension had been building up from the bottom and was beginning to break through the surface. Energy and excitement must have been moving and pulsating throughout the crowd. The whispers and anticipation were palpable and flowing from person to person. Everyone wondered if it was really true that Jesus was announcing an overthrow of the Roman government.

Thousands of years of being pushed to the very bottom by kingdom after kingdom, ruler after ruler, and finally the time for upheaval and revolt had come. The One who God promised would deliver the people from the evil, pagan forces had come, and the time was approaching when the people would join Him and prepare to take up arms. If they were to establish their kingdom and overthrow the enemy, it would be bloody. It would be violent. It would be the greatest struggle of which they had ever been a part.

Jesus began to preach about those who will join Him in His Kingdom struggle and turn everything upside-down. The Kingdom message he delivered sounded like a great role-reversal. Those at the bottom of this world would be lifted up, and those at the top would be brought down. The people at the top who had been hard-hearted and tight-fisted would finally be put in their place. The people who had been crushed by the system and who had been oppressed for so long would be liberated.

The language of Jesus may have initially sounded like fighting words to the crowd that day. Jesus was drawing a line in the sand between the haves and have nots. The order of the world needed to change and Jesus was announcing that change was imminent. In modern political speak, Jesus was giving the crowd some *red meat*, or a message against the enemy that the crowd would want to hear so as to get them fired up.

Can you imagine sitting in that crowd and hearing these words of Jesus?

If the world values accumulating, amassing, and hoarding possessions and great wealth while others are struggling to live a sustainable life, then they have already received their comfortable life and what they have will be taken away. If the world has more food than what it needs and is well-fed and over-indulgent while others are hungry, then their satisfaction and prosperity will be taken away. If the world is laughing, celebrating, and partying without giving any attention to those who are sad and mourning because of their affliction and plight, then their celebrating will turn to mourning for turning a blind eye to the brother and sister in their low position. If the world stands tall to receive the praise of men for their power, wealth, and accomplishment while those who are following the way of Jesus are insulted and rejected, then the world will experience sorrow for valuing those things that don't last and for rejecting those things that are full of life right now. The words of Jesus smacked at the powerful and wealthy oppressors, while the poor, oppressed, mournful, and beat-down crowd that day could not get enough.

Jesus said that a person is blessed, or has received divine approval, for not imitating the way of the pagan world but by living righteously on earth. The blessed live in a way that does not make sense to the systems of the world. Those in the Kingdom of God are blessed for not having much, living simply, sharing their food and possessions with each other, trusting God for their provision, and celebrating the goodness and faithfulness of God. A Kingdom life looks like following the way of Jesus in every aspect of living.

The crowds must have loved what they were hearing. If there wasn't shouting and cheering, then at least we can imagine thunderous applause. Jesus was beginning to turn the world upside-down! Those at the bottom of this world would be lifted up, and those at the top would be brought down. He was judging the enslaving and oppressive forces that had crushed and neglected the people for far too long. It was becoming more apparent each moment…the time was right for an uprising. The time was right for a revolt. The time was right for an overthrow of the pagan forces! The time was right to evict the Roman forces from their Promised Land! God's governmental and political Kingdom would be finally and completely established!

The people believed they were being mobilized and energized to follow behind their Messiah to push back the occupying forces and to finally establish God's political rule in the world. Isn't this what the prophets had prophesied about so long ago? God vindicating His chosen people? God crushing and defeating the pagan enemy forces? God reestablishing His Kingdom in Israel? The time was never better to retaliate and fight back against the enemy. And then, Jesus drops a massive bomb on the crowd.

But I say to you who hear:

Love your enemies, do good to those who hate you, bless those who curse you, pray for those who abuse you. To one who strikes you on the cheek, offer the other also, and from one who takes away your cloak do not withhold your tunic either. Give to everyone who begs from you, and from one who takes away your goods do not demand them back. And as you wish that others would do to you, do so to them.

If you love those who love you, what benefit is that to you? For even sinners love those who love them. And if you do good to those who do good to you, what benefit is that to you? For even sinners do the same. And if you lend to those from whom you expect to receive, what credit is that to you? Even sinners lend to sinners, to get back the same amount. But love your enemies, and do good, and lend, expecting nothing in return, and your reward will be great, and you will be sons of the Most High, for he is kind to the ungrateful and the evil. Be merciful, even as your Father is merciful. "Judge not, and you will not be judged; condemn not, and you will not be condemned; forgive, and you will be forgiven; give, and it will be given to you. Good measure, pressed down, shaken together, running over, will be put into your lap. For with the measure you use it will be measured back to you. Luke 6: 27-38 ESV

The World Upside-Down

All of a sudden, the message of Jesus did not sound so much like someone leading a violent revolution or overthrowing the occupying forces. It didn't even sound like the retaliatory eye-for-an-eye, tooth-for-a-tooth message that the crowd may have expected to hear. In fact, it probably sounded like a good way to continue being enslaved and crushed by the enemy. It sounded almost like a good way to stay in the same position they had been in for far too long. One wonders if some of the crowd that day would have slowly started making their way to the exits after hearing that. "Wait a second! We aren't signing up for this! We want justice! We want blood! We want revenge! We are ready to fight back and we thought you were going to lead the charge on this thing!"

Yet what the crowd heard was that Jesus wasn't interested in creating another political or violent revolution to overthrow the occupying forces. That sort of thing had been done too many times by the earthly kingdoms, and it never seemed to stop the cycle of violence. In fact, every violent revolution and every act of retaliation had always been met with more violence and more retaliation.

Allegiance

Jesus was calling on His followers to adopt a new way of living that did not operate the way the kingdoms of the world had always operated. He was calling them into a new Kingdom of complete transformation from the inside-out that would change the way they see, the way they think, and the way they would live their lives. He was calling them into a Kingdom in which the whole, healing, restorative ways of God could begin to piece back together the broken fragments of their lives and then work through them for the healing and restoration of others. Jesus was subverting and completely undercutting the political, retaliatory, eye-for-an-eye, tit-for-tat system of the world to establish God's way of living on earth. That is what He was calling His followers into, the Kingdom of God. And that is precisely what He is calling us into today.

But the way of Jesus, the way of the Kingdom of God, is lost and left untried by many of us within the Church. Instead we operate by and give our allegiance to the way of the kingdoms of the world in this matter instead of one King and one Kingdom. The truth is that whenever we are unaware of the nature of the Kingdom that Jesus preached, the Kingdom that Jesus lived out, and the Kingdom that He continues to call His followers into, we can very easily be swayed by and give our allegiance to political ideologies, captivating leaders, celebrities, popular icons, and nationalistic kingdoms of the world.

We live in a time when the allegiance to any kingdom of the world by the follower of Christ must change, and it is something that is long overdue. We have willingly been sucked into the political, nationalistic, and cultural games of our day without any hesitation. In doing so, we have compromised the very allegiance and identity we are to have *only* in Jesus Christ and His Kingdom by giving our allegiance to political ideologies and the interests of nation-states, and then assuming *their identity and their character.*

We have given our allegiance to man-made ideas and man-made governments that are as sturdy as sand. We fight, argue, defend, and spend enormous amounts of time, energy, and effort investing in those things to which we have given our allegiance. Yet, the profoundly sad and tragic truth is that we are significantly quicker to defend and fight for our life and liberty as citizens of our countries in the kingdoms of the world than we are to stand firm in our allegiance to Jesus Christ without compromising our identity in His Kingdom. Do you see the problem? We are the people sitting in the crowd that day listening to Jesus talk about the way we ought to live in the Kingdom of God, but instead of giving Him our full allegiance and following the way He calls us into, we scratch our heads and make our way to the exits. We believe it is too hard, or that it is good for Jesus but not us. All the while, the Kingdom way continues to be ignored and neglected. And being left untried, our allegiances remain mixed and our behavior compromised. It continues to be a lonely pathway of the few, rather than the sacrificial pathway of the many.

The great tragedy of the Christian is that we want to have two lovers in the same bed at the same time, but there is only room for one. We want to chase, pursue, and work hard for one lover while the other lover jealously waits for our full fidelity. We consistently compromise our marriage vows to our faithful spouse while we rampantly pursue and seductively try to charm and tame the untamable whore. She cannot be tamed, and we are mistaken if we believe otherwise.

The Christian ought not to have allegiance to or affinity toward *any* ideological, political, or governmental system in the kingdoms of the world. The Scriptures state that there is great satanic power that works in the kingdoms of the world to oppress and destroy humanity and has been working to this end from the beginning of time. *Any* system in the world may fall prey to this destructive power. That does not mean we should not pray for our leaders or our governments to exemplify God's justice and mercy in the world, but it does mean that we ought to be vigilant and stand guard against giving our allegiance to it. Our allegiance is to Lord Jesus and His Kingdom that extends the love, righteousness, justice, and mercies of God to the world. There is no other kingdom than can do that.

If history teaches us anything, it is that we ought to learn from our past so as to not make the same mistakes again. As such, history ought to give caution and pause to Christians who put their hope, faith, and trust in any ideological, political, or governmental system. The late Art Katz recounted the relationship and affinity German Jews had to the cultural, scientific, and economic development of Germany:

> [We] were so deeply ensconced as Germans with a 2000-year tenure in Germany, though we were Jews…the fact of the matter was that we were more German than we were Jewish. And though the dark clouds gathered, we could not believe what they indicated. And we said, in that human way that does not want to recognize painful things, "This too shall pass." The tragic thing was…it didn't.
>
> And who could have imagined that the land of Beethoven, Hegel, Nitsche, Schopenhauer, Gerda, and Schiller could be the land of the systematic annihilation of the Jewish people. It was inconceivable. And because the Jews were so taken up with the virtue of German civilization, they became its victim. **They themselves had participated in the creation of the monster…and were instrumental in creating the very civilization that destroyed them.**[31]

I do not want to insinuate that the situation of the Christian is in any way like the plight or suffering of the Jewish Holocaust victims. But this recounting should be a very appropriate caution and lesson for the Christian who has been instrumental and influential in the development of his or her country. It should further give us pause to the fact that, while we ought to only have one allegiance to Jesus Christ and His Kingdom, we could very well be devoured by the very entity that we helped create and in which we have put our faith. Do we not see that putting our faith in any political movement or governmental entity or any kingdom of the world, rather than the Kingdom of God, is ultimately a dead-end road?

We are told not to put our faith in those things of earth that can be shaken. Rather, we are called to put our complete trust in that which will *never* be shaken.[32] So let us only give our allegiance to the King and the Kingdom that will never be shaken, and let us learn the secret of being content in any and all situations while demonstrating the love, justice, and mercies of God to the world.

The Kingdom of God

The Kingdom that Jesus preached and established was one that operated by a new set of values, a new way of thinking, a new way of being human. This Kingdom of God was like nothing the world had ever known or seen before. As such, Jesus was not preoccupied with fighting violently against the kingdoms of the world or the prevailing governmental or political order. *Jesus wasn't even preoccupied with trying to reform them.* In fact, maybe to the shock of many in the audience that day and maybe to you as well, *He was not even preoccupied with trying to establish a new or different political or governmental system.* He was certainly not trying to build up a bricks and mortar palace where He would rule from the top-down.

The Kingdom that Jesus came to proclaim would be established much differently than the kingdoms of the world, and it would not look like anything the world had ever seen because the people in this Kingdom would do everything opposite from the ways and workings of the world. It would be a grassroots, organic movement that changes the world from the bottom-up and from the inside-out, defying every bit of worldly wisdom in the process.

When the world hits you, do not retaliate but give the other cheek. When the world is weighing you down with heavy requests, don't just go one mile with the request but go two miles. When the world takes everything you have, even the coat off of your back, don't just give your coat but go even further by offering your shirt. When the way of the world harbors anger and holds grudges, be one who forgives your friends and your enemies alike. Don't just forgive once, but forgive and forgive and forgive.

When the world is quick to respond and rip a person to shreds, be one who controls your anger and the words that come from your mouth. When the world devalues relationships and marriages, be one who looks to the interest of others, honors commitments, and always remains selfless. When the world looks out for and protects its own pursuits and interests to the detriment of others, be one who treats others as you would want to be treated yourself. When the world casts the stone of judgment at the sinner, be one who loves and stands beside every single person without judgment. When the world shuns the outcast and pushes him to the edges of society, be one who befriends the outcast and welcomes him back into loving and healing community.

When the world lords over you with power and authority, be one who serves with the utmost humility. When the world takes the seat of honor so it can be seen and noticed by everyone, be one who takes the seat of low-position in the back of the room. When the world puts on a show of being pure and good but is corrupt at the very core, be one who is pure from the inside and let it work out through your life. When the world continues in the ways of injustice and is merciless to the least in society, be one who stands for the least and for those who cannot defend themselves by demanding justice and mercy.

When the world fights and wars among themselves, be one who always stands on the side of peace no matter the situation and no matter the circumstance. When the world insults, ridicules, and curses you, be one who blesses in return. When the evil of the world assaults you, be the one who does not resist the evil. And when the world beats you, spits upon you, and is preparing to crucify you, continue on the way of forgiveness and self-sacrificial love.

That is the Kingdom of God! That is the treasure of great riches that the world so desperately needs. That is the pearl of great value for which we sell everything we have in order to attain it. That is what will spread like an infection, a mustard seed, yeast in the dough if the world would ever hear it and see it put into practice by a transformed people. That is the in-breaking of heaven into the house that has been held hostage for far too long. That is the occupation, proclamation, task, and obsession of the follower of Christ in the vineyard of the world!

The Kingdom of God is the full-on reign of God in the hearts and minds of those who believe in the way, life, and teachings of Jesus. The Kingdom of God is embodied by those who have died to the old, tired, and worn-out ways of the world, and who have been made new by the working and empowering of the Spirit of God in order to bring heaven on earth, while awaiting and anticipating the return of Christ as Lord at the renewal of all things!!!

The Kingdom of God is what a life looks like when God reigns in and through a person here on earth in every single thought, action, attitude, situation, or scenario. It looks like an invasion from heaven into the strongholds of a person's life, a cleaning out of the house, a light breaking through into the darkness, and a constant and continual in-breaking of heaven through one's life into the world. It is a Kingdom that reigns in the hearts and minds of people, not through the political, governmental, bureaucratic, religious, institutional brick and mortar systems of the world. The Kingdom of God *will never* come through those systems because they will all pass away one day.

That is why Jesus said that the Kingdom of God is not something that can be seen or observed. It is not visible with the eye. In fact, people will not be able to say, "Here it is," or "There it is," because the Kingdom of God is within the hearts and minds of those who follow the way, life, and teachings of Jesus.[33] In this way, the Kingdom of God can not be conquered, destroyed, or defeated, but it continues to grow larger and to spread from person to person all throughout the world. There is not a savage, a soldier, a maniac, a terrorist, or a world army on the face of this planet that can pin it down or extinguish it because it is growing, it is spreading and it is all consuming. The Kingdom of God is breaking into our world like an infection to displace the kingdoms of the world and to establish the reign of God, through and through, in the hearts, minds, and lives of people who are like Jesus in everything we do. And, it is this Kingdom to which we are being called right now.

Revolution of Love

The offensive that the follower of Jesus undertakes is one of revolutionary love. It is the kind of love that looks like Jesus Christ in every situation, good and bad, even to the point that it may cost us our lives. Yes, you read that correctly, *even to the point of costing your life!* Let me be clear again, the Kingdom of God never moves forward violently, but only through selfless, sacrificial love. It is love put on display in such a selfless and radical way that it lays itself down for friends and enemies alike.

If one hundred Christians were asked if they agree with the teaching of Jesus to love their enemies, each one of them would agree with it. Yet when it comes to actually loving their enemies in real life, far fewer agree. I sent a good friend of mine a text message recently that read, "It is only when one has decided he can lay down his life for his enemy that he can be called a Christian. Consequently, there are few Christians in our churches." In response my friend texted, "Lay down their lives for their enemies? Most 'Christians' would not lay down their sandwich." This kind of poignant truth is disheartening.

I was at a business meeting recently in Chicago. One evening I went to a Mexican restaurant with some of my business colleagues. After a really good dinner and conversation we began our trek back to the hotel. My three colleagues were in deep conversation about guns and firing ranges. Since I didn't have much to offer to the conversation I spaced out and started thinking about other things. That was until one of the men started talking about how he carries a concealed weapon to church service each week. He went on to say that his church recently implemented security measures for their church services. At any one time there are at least three people…with guns…at their church service! Can you imagine the early Church, during a time in which they suffered the greatest violence, abandoning the way of Christ by picking up arms for fear of their lives at their church service!? *The main reason why we as Christian can demonstrate the self-sacrificial love of Christ to the world is because we do not have to fear death!* The cross that Christ would have us bear for each person in the world is love. It is a love that lays down its life for both friend and enemy.

But again, according to the so-called wisdom of the world and unfortunately many within our churches, the approach of non-retaliation and sacrificial love is a failed strategy. In the way that the world system operates, it does not work or make sense. Even further, you will not find one book in the world on fighting, modern warfare, or the art of war that would ever suggest such a ridiculous strategy for the defeat of an enemy. In the wisdom of the world, self-sacrificial love will always result in defeat.

The fact of the matter is, however, that this strategy has been tried at least one time, and it worked brilliantly. It is *precisely and exactly* that strategy and model to which Jesus has called each of us. The follower of Jesus should live such an uncompromising life in the Kingdom of God that not even the threat of death itself will shake this Kingdom. Love will always, always, always prevail in a Kingdom life, even and most especially when it is face to face with death itself. Love always wins. Love is always victorious. Love never fails.

So why should it surprise the Christian that self-sacrificial love is exactly in line with the rest of this upside-down Kingdom that Jesus announced? The cross, representing the ugliest, most hateful, and barbaric form of human suffering and punishment was completely turned upside-down through the humble submission and self-sacrificial love of Jesus Christ to become the greatest symbol of humble submission and self-sacrificial love this world has ever witnessed! People do not wear the crucifix around their necks because it represents barbaric torture. They wear it because it has come to represent the greatest sacrifice of love ever demonstrated in a human life! It is the way of Jesus Christ. It is the way of the Kingdom of God. And, it is the way of the follower of Christ.

But the way of Jesus, once again, is left untried because it doesn't make sense to us. From our limited human perspective, we have been convinced that it is good for Jesus but not for His followers. I have news for you: it is the *only* way that the forces of evil, hatred, and death can be undermined and defeated once and for all; it is through humble and self-sacrificial love demonstrated through our lives for the world to see. The same power that raised this Jesus to life is the same exact power we have been given to extend the Kingdom of God over and against the powers and principalities of evil! So what do we have to fear?

It is only through that kind of power and that kind of love that evil, hatred, violence, and even death will once and for all be completely exhausted. Self-sacrificial love cannot be extinguished, pressed down, crushed, or defeated, and the forces of evil will *never* find victory precisely because of that. For it was in the greatest moment of sacrificial love the world has ever seen that death prematurely proclaimed the greatest victory, and then met its greatest defeat. Death lost its sting when it was triumphed by resurrection! It is in the resurrection that those who put their faith in Jesus have the assurance that death is only a moment of sleep until we are resurrected to new life, receiving resurrection bodies that will never perish again. The Christian can move forward in confidence that death does not win, only love does. That is the reason we move forth only in love.

It is now that the salvation and power of the Kingdom of God through the authority of Jesus Christ has come! The great treasure of the Kingdom of God has been found, unearthed, and opened for all to see! The adversary who accuses the children of God both day and night, who has been hurled down, and he who has enslaved all of God's good creation to sin and death has been defeated and is gasping for his final breath. The enemy is overcome by the blood of Jesus Christ and by the very testimony of the followers of Jesus, the new creation people, the Body of Christ! And we do not love our lives so much as to shrink away from death![34] Praise God!

CHAPTER 8

THE KINGDOM BREAKING OUT

A branch cannot be broken off from a vine and survive. It will soon lose its nourishment, begin to dry and crack, and then slowly waste away. However if a branch stays connected to the vine, it will receive nourishment and will bear fruit. It is with the images of vines, branches, and fruit that Jesus conveyed the power He would give to those who are connected to Him and through whom He would do His work. Jesus said those who are connected to Him will bear fruit in their lives. He is the vine, we are the branches. If we remain in Him, then His power will work through us to produce fruit in our lives and to extend His Kingdom throughout the world.[35]

But if this power is going to break out through our lives and ultimately transform the world, we have to get out of the way. That is why the pattern for the follower of Jesus centers on the death and resurrection. It is the pattern for the individual in the dying of the old self and the resurrecting to new life, becoming a new creation through the Holy Spirit. As we die to the old ways of life that previously rebelled against God, we are resurrected to a new life in which His power prevails. We become the means through which the Kingdom of God breaks into the world. It is only through the pattern of death and resurrection that the follower of Jesus can be used by God as a means to transform the Church and establish his Kingdom reign.

By connecting to the true source of Life, like branches connecting to the vines, we become Christ to the world in such an uncompromising and compelling way that nothing, especially death, can keep us from marching into enemy-occupied territory and breaking down the gates of hell to extend the great treasure of the Kingdom of God throughout the entire world and into the hearts and minds of everyone we meet.

So What Are We Doing?

Based on the appearance of those who claim to follow Jesus, we don't look like a group of people up for such a task. When you compare who we are and what we have been doing in our churches to whom we ought to be and what we ought to be doing as the Body of Christ, it is very overwhelming and burdensome. It is what breaks my heart, causes me to be restless, and makes me doubt those whom God has trusted for such a task. We are some ragtag bunch of people! We continue to run after dead-end pursuits, grinning and giggling, while the great task awaits us.

It reminds me of a situation one summer when I was scrambling to find a job to earn some extra money for college in the fall. I went to a temp agency and told them that I would take the first job that became available. The next morning I received a phone call and was told to show up at a job site where a construction company was building a family restaurant.

When I arrived at the site I found out that the foreman and his entire crew had walked off of the job the day before. Neither I nor the other five temp workers had done much construction work in the past. I can't really remember how long we stood around and looked at each other in confusion before we asked what we were supposed to be doing, but I am sure it was quite some time. We were in way over our heads with the task and didn't even know where to begin. Finally someone showed up and gave us some guidance. We were still quite shaky on the job, but the work was being done. In utter amazement, we finished the task through to completion. In fact, to my knowledge that fine establishment still stands today!

Those of us in our churches are like temp workers. We have been hired for a job that we do not have the skills to do, nor do we know what skills are even required to do the job. We have spent so much of our time on other unrelated tasks, either handed down through the generations or others we have acquired on our own, that we really do not know where to begin. Sure we can swing an occasional hammer or saw an occasional board, but we are lacking the all-around know-how to complete the task. There is no doubt that we could use some much needed guidance. Maybe that is why we spend so much time in our churches talking about the work rather than doing it- because we don't know how to do it or where to begin.

If we have been given the task of invading enemy-occupied territory, breaking down the gates of hell, and taking back that which is rightfully God's, how exactly do we do that? Where would we even begin? What does that even look like in practice? How do we go from spiritual weaklings who are preoccupied with dead-end pursuits to mighty spiritual giants whom God uses to clean up the house before His arrival? The answer to our questions is found in the most unexpected and exciting places. It is in our worship.

Rethinking Worship

Before you begin rolling your eyes, thinking you have a good grasp on worship, or before you begin dismissing such a preposterous beginning point, I would ask you to just pause and breathe for a second. Worship is not what you think it is, what we believe it to be in our churches, or what Contemporary Christian Music told you it is. In fact, once we have a clearer vision of what exactly worship is, it will change your life, change your church, and then it will begin to change everything.

In the New Testament, the predominant Greek word used for worship is *proskuneo*. *Proskuneo* means to lie prostrate before someone who is worthy. Did you get that? It means to take your entire body and lie flat with your face pressed to the ground in submission before one who is worthy. You will notice that the word *proskuneo* did not mention anything about singing.

With that sort of understanding about worship, it sounds quite different than what we have ever been told. That kind of worship sounds selfless. That kind of worship sounds sacrificial. That kind of worship makes me think that I need to understand my position before this Worthy One. That kind of worship reminds me that I am simply dirt with Divine breath. That kind of worship makes it sound like it has nothing to do with *my* wants, needs, and desires, because I have set them aside for this One who is Worthy.

The one lying down with his or her face pressed to the floor becomes less, and the One who is Worthy becomes more. At the most basic level worship is, "the believer's response of all that they are - mind, emotions, will, body - to what God is and says and does."[36] Our worship is a complete emptying of ourselves of our own wants, needs, and desires in sacrifice, so as to be filled by the One who is Worthy. We become the branch connected to the vine, receiving nourishment and power to produce spiritual fruit. All of a sudden worship doesn't seem so much like an interchangeable word for music and singing as much as a position that gets *me* out of the way and opens the door for God's Glory to finally be welcomed to work through my entire life and to break out into the world in power!

It is through our worship that we become a vessel, a conduit, filled by the Holy Spirit of God extending outward into the world. Our worship is us getting out of the way so the Spirit of God can work through our hands, our legs, our voices, and our entire bodies for His Kingdom purposes in the world. Through our worship, we become the point where God meets a hurting world in need of healing and restoring. The gates of hell are broken down and the works of Satan are destroyed because the Holy Spirit is on the offensive. We become the means through which the Kingdom of God breaks into existence on earth.

Worship is the beginning point of how the battle is fought. We get out of the way and let the Spirit work through us to fight the powers and principalities of evil. Again, when Paul writes that our battle is not against flesh and blood but against the powers and principalities of evil, how do you think that battle is fought?[37] It is not by fighting and beating down other human beings; it is through our worship. It is by our selfish, carnal selves getting out of the way and inviting the Spirit of God to work in us, through us, and around us in such power that the enemy forces are pushed back and exhausted. We become a living sacrifice, continually sacrificing our own wants, needs, and desires so as to become a walking, breathing vessel of God's blessing, healing, love, and transformation in the world.

However, taking on a life of worship is not as easy as it sounds. That may seem obvious being that we have missed the point of worship for so long by twisting and turning it into a mass heap of syrupy and trite confusion. We have turned worship into something completely opposite from what it ought to be. If our worship is about each of us humbling ourselves and sacrificing our wants, needs, and desires so that God can work and move through our lives, then how did worship become *all about us and what we think we need to get out of it anyway?*

Consumer-Driven Worship

We have become church-consumers and our churches work to satisfy our needs. Our churches cater stylistically to those of the traditional worship persuasion, the contemporary worship persuasion, and the post-modern worship persuasion. We even have a "blended" worship service for those who can't make up their minds. Even further, there are churches that advertise through their church name what type of worship they have. There is a church close to my hometown that is called The Country Gospel Music church. I am not kidding!

Our understanding of and participation in worship has become so completely self-indulgent, so self-focused, and so wildly driven by our own individual wants, needs, and desires that it has to begin to change! We cannot continue down this consumer-driven path within the Church. Our worship is *not about us*, but about the One who is worthy and is looking for empty vessels to fill. We must become living sacrifices that are holy and pleasing to God because that is the most essential act of worship. We must sacrifice ourselves. We must sacrifice our wants, needs, and desires. We must sacrifice the ways of the old life and become something that is usable by God for His Kingdom purposes.

It is when we finally get out of the way and submit to the Spirit of God that the war can be fought. It is when we finally beat our bodies into submission that we finally stop obstructing the in-breaking Kingdom. It is when we decide to leave the slavery of self-indulgence, pass through the cleansing waters, and break into freedom that we can be led by a towering pillar of clouds by day and a mighty pillar of fire by night.

Becoming a Sacrifice

Few have considered that following the way of Christ involves personal sacrifice. We believe that once we are on the team it is a matter of title and association rather than a matter of sacrifice, submission, and transformation. We throw all kinds of words around in our churches that become so commonplace and casual they lose their meaning.

Take a word like *repentance.* The Greek word for repentance is *metanoia*. *Metanoia* means transformation. It is a changing. It is an evolving. It is a continual movement from the life that was previously lived into a life of new creation. But at the heart of *metanoia* is personal sacrifice. It is a sacrifice of the old ways and a taking on of the new ways. Lives of sacrifice can be nothing short of a complete transformation. But while everyone in the church nods his or her head in agreement that repentance is necessary for a Christian, few in the Church live as if they have been transformed.

How will this transformation ever happen if we do not get out of the way so as to let in the power of Christ through the Holy Spirit? How will we become this new creation people if the Spirit continues to hit the brick wall of our inflated egos and self-interest? How will we ever be people of *metanoia* if we remain hard-hearted and unchanged? How will the Spirit move out and into the world if we are not a people of sacrificial worship? How will the Kingdom of God invade and then break out in our lives if we are not people of sacrificial worship? How will we ever learn that following Christ, taking on his yoke, and becoming His disciple involves personal sacrifice if our churches only stay at the surface with feel good messages that increase numbers, but never call us into personal sacrifice? The answer is that nothing will change unless we learn to be sacrificial followers of Christ.

There is profound wisdom in pursuing a life in which we are called to sacrifice everything. Only there will we end up with *nothing...and everything.* Christ died and resurrected so that we should no longer live to ourselves but live only for Him. We carry around in our bodies the death and resurrection of Jesus.[38] We continually sacrifice ourselves in the death of our own ways, so that the life of Jesus, the Resurrection, the Kingdom of God, the full-on Reign of God may be revealed in our daily lives.

It is essential that we begin to learn how to carry the cross of Christ around in our bodies every moment of the day, crucifying the old man when he rears his ugly head. We must learn how to put the carnal and sinful ways of the body to death. We must learn how to put the corrupt urges, tendencies, and misgivings of the body into complete subjection and control to the Holy Spirit. We must put to death in our bodies the old ways of sexual perversion, lust, drunkenness, idolatry of possessions, anger, hatred, resentment, selfishness, self-centeredness, division, disunity, gossip, envy, conflict, and all those things of our bodies that keep us from being used by God in mighty and miraculous ways.[39] It is only when we have allowed the Spirit of God to take full control of our lives that we will be clothed for battle with the breastplate of righteousness, the belt of truth, the helmet of salvation, the shield of faith, and the shoes of peace.[40] It is only then that we will be prepared to fight the battle against the powers and principalities of evil.

But putting to death the sinful desires, inclinations, and misgivings of the wayward body is more than just thinking about it. As an athlete enters into strict training to prepare for the race, so the follower of Jesus must enter into strict training to be fit for the battle. We do not just run around in circles aimlessly, swinging and waving our arms in the air.[41] We move forward in discipleship and strict training, beating our bodies into full submission to the Holy Spirit.

So our worship is a sacrifice of ourselves and a filling of the Holy

Spirit. We worship every moment of the day by prostrating ourselves, humbling ourselves, and giving way to the Worthy One. As a way to live sacrificially in our worship, the follower of Jesus takes on a life of spiritual discipline that trains us in the way of Christ and helps us find victory over the tendencies and misgivings of the sinful, carnal flesh.

Sacrifice Through Discipline

There are greater books that explain the life of spiritual discipline in which the Christian enters, and I would fall painfully short in trying to say what they have already said so beautifully, so simply, and so practically. For that reason, if you have not read *Celebration of Discipline* by Richard Foster, *The Spirit of the Disciplines* by Dallas Willard, or *The Cost of Discipleship* by Deitrich Bonhoeffer I would highly suggest you do so. You will find beautiful gifts from God in the pages of those classic Christian works. But I would also be amiss to not at least offer some insight on a couple of the spiritual disciplines that will begin to help us walk the way of sacrificial worship by putting our bodies under the authority of the Holy Spirit.

Let me be clear. Entering into a life of spiritual discipline is not an end in itself. It is a means through which we begin down the path of a sacrificial living. When we look at Christ, His disciples, and the early Church, we see people who practiced many spiritual disciplines as a means of submission to the Spirit of God in their daily lives. They were people who practiced prayer, solitude and silence, fasting, confession, frugality, and many other disciplines in order to give themselves completely over to the Spirit dwelling within them and to worship God with their entire lives, making themselves a means through which God could work and move in power.

While I would love to unpack the benefit of all the disciplines in our lives, I am only going to touch on a couple of them to make the point of how spiritual discipline can allow the Holy Spirit to work and move powerfully in our own lives. As we begin discussing two of the spiritual disciplines, confession and fasting, please do not think that with a snap of the finger your life will be changed. Taking on a life of spiritual discipline indicates that we are a work in progress. We are people who are being refined. We are people who are being transformed. We are the people of *metanoia*. It is the sacrificial path that we take to become less in our own lives, so that God may become more. We are living sacrifices, people of *proskuneo*, people who humbly submit to God the Spirit in everything we do. Therefore, the spiritual disciplines are worshipful acts of submission to the ways and workings of the Spirit. So to that end, let us look at the disciplines of confession and fasting.

Confession

There may be no better place to begin a life of worship, sacrifice, and submission than with the spiritual discipline of confession. Please don't run for the hills just yet. If you are not familiar with confession or only believe it to be an old, stale religious tradition, please hang with me. While it is the most misunderstood of all spiritual disciplines, it is also the spiritual discipline that can remove the barrier of sin that separates us from God and our brothers and sisters in Christ. Confession opens up the dark, hidden sinful areas of our lives so that the Light of Christ may invade.

Confession is simply recognizing and verbalizing all the ways that we miss the mark of being this new creation. It is recognizing and verbalizing all the ways that we still think, act, and behave like the old man who was once nailed to the cross, but who continues to creep back into our lives. It is recognizing and verbalizing each way that we still operate by the ways and workings of the kingdoms of the world. Confession is the beginning point of repentance, *metanoia,* or transformation.

In the New Testament book of James the follower of Christ is told *confess your sins one to another, and pray for one another, and then you will be healed.*[42] But many become indignant at this point offering that they *only* need to confess their sins to God. While it is true that God and God alone grants forgiveness for our waywardness and it is always good and appropriate to confess our sins to God, confession is more than just seeking forgiveness from God. It is the power of God working through a community of believers to begin the healing and restoring of the wayward sinner in grace, love, and patience. Confession to one another is a powerful reminder to the Christian community that not one of us can take a high position above another because we are all at the foot of the cross together as sinners.

Sin is bent on dividing, fracturing, and breaking. Sin breaks us away from wholeness and unity with God and takes us into places of isolation away from whole and complete unity with Christian community. Confession to God and your Christian brother or sister removes the barrier of sin, taking you out of isolation and into loving, accepting, whole, and healed community. In confession, you finally realize that you are not alone in your sin and that you are not the only sinner. Confession takes you from a high position of judgment, believing that others sins are worse than yours, to a low position of humility when you recognize that your sins are the same as your brother's sin. Confession takes you from the position above the cross where you have hammered the nails into the hands and feet of the sinner for far too long, to a place below the cross where all join together to be covered by the forgiving and healing blood of Christ. It is in confession that the broken vessel begins to be put back together for the uses and purposes of God on earth.

Although I will go into greater detail in the final chapter about my story of the power of confession, I do want to say that it wasn't until the last two years that I discovered the healing power that is found in confession to God and my Christian brothers. After a few friends and I had read *The Cost of Discipleship* and had taken to heart the writings of James, we committed to meeting weekly, confessing our sins to one another and taking the Lord's Supper. We could no longer hide behind the plants and shrubs, away from God and others, trying to cover our nakedness.[43] We stood before God and each other, naked and exposed. The power and stranglehold of the old man began to lose strength as we carried him to the cross together. Kneeling at the foot of the cross we prayed for the Spirit of God to fill us and transform us into the likeness of Christ. Through our confession to God and to our Christian brothers or sisters and through the prayers of the righteous, we are forgiven, healed, and made whole. That is precisely what we began to experience.

That is the wisdom found in the words of James. Confess your sins one to another, praying for each other, and then you will be healed, *iaomai,* made whole and complete. Confession begins healing and making whole that which was fractured, broken, and out of alignment. Confession begins uniting that which was previously running in rebellion. Confession begins to restore the *shalom* of God in and through the life of the Christian. Confession opens the doorway for the Spirit to reign in the tendencies, compulsions, and misgivings of the flesh. Confession is the great announcement to God and the world that even in you, Christ is making all things new!

Fasting

If the Christian has been reluctant to confess his or her sins to one another, the Christian has been completely ignorant and lacking in the spiritual discipline of fasting. The sad reality is that the average Christian not only knows very little about the discipline of fasting, but has never taken it on as an essential spiritual discipline. We hear about fasting and relegate it to the spiritual giants who do it when things get really serious, but we do not believe that fasting is actually a practice of the "average" Christian. While we dismiss this essential discipline, we continue to be ignorant of the spiritual effect this discipline can have on us.

It should not be lost on us that fasting was a common practice of Jesus and his followers. In fact, Jesus instructed his followers, "*When* you fast, don't look somber like the hypocrites."[44] The assumption is that…we fast. In another instance, Jesus responded to some naysayers who complained that His disciples were not fasting by saying, "How can the guests of the bridegroom mourn while he is with them? The time will come when the bridegroom will be taken from them; *then they will fast*."[45] With such an expectation around fasting, it is essential for us to understand how *not eating food* disciplines the body and puts it in total submission to the Spirit.

There is nothing more central to the life of a human being than food. From the time we are born, we eat. Our body is dependent on nourishment to function and thrive, and so we continue to eat daily. When a person does not eat for a time, the body responds. The stomach complains and growls as a constant reminder that it needs food. It doesn't matter what we are doing, the longer we keep food from this grumpy organ, the sounds go from whispers to groans. So, we feed it to make it happy (and to quiet it down). A person who is aware of what just happened knows that the body just dictated the terms of the deal, or that your stomach just told you what it wanted and you obeyed it.

But what if the Christian was not controlled by this body of sin? What if there was a way to not be controlled by the urges, tendencies, and compulsions of the body? Where would one start? Where would one begin? It would start by consciously taking away one of the most basic needs of the body…food.

The body again begins throwing a tantrum. It begins screaming, "I need…I need…I want…I want!" But the Christian resolute in the discipline of fasting responds, "Body, you are not in control of me. You do not dictate the terms of this deal. I do not obey you. The Spirit is in control of my life, and you do not have power over me." Fasting puts your body in subjection to the Spirit that controls you. The Christian has taken the first step at becoming aware of how much the body's urges, tendencies, and compulsions dictate his or her actions and behavior.

A Breakthrough

This awareness and discipline is critical. It is critical for the man who has urges to look at pornography. It is critical for the woman who can not buy enough and is never satisfied with what she has. It is critical for the person who is overweight and is controlled by an unending appetite for more food. It is critical for the person controlled by laziness, envy, addiction, anger, retaliation, anxiety, worry, and getting in the last word. Fasting allows the Spirit to change the person, allowing the light to break through the darkness. The desires of the body have been put to rest, and the desires of the Spirit abound in freedom. This is the kind of fasting that God requires of you, fasting that changes your life.

It is when we are no longer controlled by the self-seeking desires of this natural body that the power of God begins to work in our lives for spiritual transformation. When our minds and our entire lives are set on those things of the Spirit, rather than the fleeting and dead-end pursuits of our bodies, our desires become what the Spirit desires. We no longer hunger for the things that satisfy our carnal cravings rather for those things of the Spirit. We are God's new creation. We are the vessel through which the Kingdom of God reigns and extends on earth.

All of a sudden prayer is no longer a dead-end ritual or an obligation, but words of unceasing exaltation and devotion that are expressed into existence with every breath. Our praise becomes the power that pushes back the forces of evil in the lives of those around us and extends God's Kingdom on earth as it is in heaven. Serving others with our hands is the power of God breaking down strongholds and invading enemy space. Every mile we walk with our legs to visit the orphaned and widowed tramples and destroys the work of the enemy. Every word and testimony spoken into existence joins the power of the blood of Christ to defeat the enemy once and for all. Our sacrificial worship is the means through which the spiritual battle is fought. It is where the strongholds of the enemy are crushed and defeated and the healing, life, love, beauty, and creativity break forth in such power that the kingdoms of the world become the Kingdom of God.

Through our worshipful act of confession, the Spirit begins to heal and mend back together we who are broken, divided, and separated from

God and our brothers and sisters in Christ. Through our worshipful act of fasting, we who have been made whole and healed put our carnal and selfish desires in subjection to the Holy Spirit to begin working through us from the inside-out. We are truly the vines connected securely to the Branch of nourishment and strength. It is through our sacrificial lives of worship that we receive the strength and power of the Spirit to become usable by God for the transformation of the Church for the sake of the world.

CHAPTER 9

THE KINGDOM UNITED

We move outward and onward into the world, into the streets, announcing from every street corner that the great treasure of the Kingdom of God that the world has needed has been found. We move outward and onward through our worship as the servants of humanity demonstrating a self-sacrificial love the world has never before seen. We move outward and onward in spiritual discipline beating our bodies into submission so as to be a vessel that the Spirit of God can use to break out into the world. And finally, we move outward and onward as the Body of Christ *united*...yes, finally *united and one*...to wage the final battle against the Adversary and the powers and principalities that have enslaved us for far too long, so as to make ready the Kingdom for the coming Lord of all lords.

It is for the proclamation and demonstration of the Kingdom of God that the Body of Christ is finally united to complete our task. We join together as One to preach the message of the Kingdom to the world through our words and through our lives. Anything less than marching forward together under one Lordship or moving together as One Body directed by the headship of Christ is completely unacceptable.

The Shame of the Church

Disunity is the embarrassment and the ridicule of the Church. We have been mocked by the cynics and the naysayers who declare that there is no way that God exists because if He did, there would not be such a divided and misaligned group of people who claim to work on His behalf. Disunity is the dark stain, the blemish, on that which is to be pure and spotless. Of all people who ought to know something about unity, we are the exact opposite of it. The Church is *the* group of people who has become the face of pettiness, division, in-fighting, conflict, and war with each other. Our disunity is nothing less than shameful and disgraceful. The grace and peace of God that has been so generously given to us and that we should generously and freely extend to each other has instead been replaced by judgment and conflict.

While we all agree that Jesus is Lord and we confess Him with our lips, our denominations and individual churches argue and compete *against* each other as if we are on separate teams involved in some sort of competition. We behave as if our individual churches or denominations have been given the *exact* truth or revelation from God and we are the *only* bearers of it. We treat other brothers and sisters in Christ as heretical pagans if they do one small thing differently than we do. All the while we continue to divide and divide and divide, and build walls higher and higher and higher.

Brothers and sisters, what are you trying to hold on to and defend? What kingdom or power structure are you building up and trusting in? Can you not see that you are fighting the wrong enemy and your division works against the Kingdom of God? Do you continue to argue for your "right" position because it glorifies *you* or glorifies *God*? These are tough questions, but questions that have to be asked nonetheless. Is it about your own kingdom or the Kingdom of God?

Do we all not preach Christ crucified and resurrected? Do we all not preach that through our faith in Jesus we are saved? Do we all not preach the confession and the repentance of sin? Do we all not preach one faith and one baptism? Do we all not take a bread and cup that unites us into one body through One Body? Do we not believe the words of Jesus that a kingdom divided against itself ***will not*** stand! This is true for *any* kingdom. How will you bear graciously and patiently with your enemy if you cannot bear graciously and patiently with your Christian brother or sister?

Prayer of Unity

While I have had people laugh at my optimism of the Church coming together in unity, I do not view the call to unity as some wishy-washy, pie-in-the-sky, lofty idea that makes everyone feel good but has no chance of happening. In fact, I believe it will happen in this generation. The call to unity as the Body of Christ in the world *will* happen and it *will* be an answer to prayer. It will not only be an answer to *my* prayer, but it will be the answer to the prayer of *Jesus Christ* himself.

It was in the last documented prayer of Jesus just before He was arrested that He prayed for all those who believe and follow Him, and it was a prayer for unity among them.

> My prayer is not for [the disciples] alone. I pray also for those who will believe in me through their message, that all of them may be one, Father, just as you are in me and I am in you. May they also be in us so that the world may believe that you have sent me. I have given them the glory that you gave me, that they may be one as we are one: I in them and you in me. May they be brought to complete unity to let the world know that you sent me and have loved them even as you have loved me. Father, I want those you have given me to be with me where I am, and to see my glory, the glory you have given me because you loved me before the creation of the world. Righteous Father, though the world does not know you, I know you, and they know that you have sent me. I have made you known to them, and will continue to make you known in order that the love you have for me may be in them and that I myself may be in them. John 17: 20-26

The prayer of Jesus is a prayer for perfect submission, perfect relationship, and perfect unity with God and each other so as to make this unity complete. Through Jesus we have been given the glory that we may be One, as Jesus and the Father are One. It is through His glory given to us that we can believe complete unity is possible and will happen, only in His power, not ours.

However, it is our inability to be united that sends a profound message to the world that Jesus was not sent by God! It is our disunity that obstructs the love of Christ from being conveyed to the entire world. How do you like that? Seriously, *how do you like that?* Because of our petty disagreements, differences of opinion, selfish hearts and attitudes, and our unwillingness to extend grace and peace to our brothers and sisters who call Jesus as Lord, we undermine the extension of God's love to the world!

If ever there was a reason that the Church ought to pursue unity and become known once again as the united Body of Christ, it is to send a loud and emphatic message to the world that Jesus *was* sent by the Father.

And the reason he was sent was to destroy the works of Satan, rescue all of creation, and establish the reign of God in the hearts and minds of those who believe in him so as to extend and restore peace and love throughout the entire created order.

To a jaded and cynical world, the message is only as credible and believable as the messenger. And the Church will not be a credible and believable messenger of the Kingdom of God until the prayer of Jesus is realized and the Church united. Will you and your church be the answer to Jesus' prayer of unity for all believers and join in the great Kingdom work in the world, or will you continue to undermine the great Kingdom work that needs to be done only to build up and trust in your own kingdom?

The Way of Disunity

A friend of mine asked me what kind of books I read. I told her that I read dry, boring theology books that she would not be interested in reading. She paused for a second and then said, "Actually, I would like to read some books like that because I have a lot of questions and I am trying to figure things out." I asked her what it was exactly that she was trying to figure out. She went on to tell me a story that makes my point about disunity loud and clear.

She and her husband came from different Christian church denominations. So instead of going to either of their denominations once they were married, they decided to choose one that neither one of them had grown up in. One Sunday, and without getting into all the sensitive specifics of the incident that happened, they joined together at their new church with their extended families.

At one point during the church service, my friend's mother-in-law began crying hysterically, telling my friend and her husband that what they were doing in their church was wrong and that all of them were going to hell as a result. The mother-in-law made such a scene and caused so much commotion that my friend decided at that moment that there is no way that Christianity could be true. She concluded that there was no way that there could be so many denominations with such a wide spectrum of beliefs if Christianity were true. She also concluded that there was certainly no way that a true follower of Christ would unleash such an unwarranted and hateful response to another person if Christianity were true.

The truth of the matter is that we are all imperfect people trying to do our very best for God. We are all in error on one thing or another. There is not one person in this world who can claim to have the full knowledge and revelation of God nailed down exactly. I am sorry…there isn't. If you think you are that person then you need to be the first person in the confession line for lying. The smartest and most Spirit-led theologians in the world debate back and forth just trying to uncover a little more truth, but they would be the first people to say that there is so much we do not know, and I agree.

Take for example the ongoing debate between John Piper and N.T. Wright about the doctrine of justification. Many of you reading this may not know either of these men, not to mention that you may not know exactly what they are debating or why it even matters. Both men are followers of Jesus who do scholarly biblical work as well as pastoral work within their respective churches. Each man has reached very different conclusions about the word "justification" that Paul uses in the book of Romans. Both men are incredibly intelligent. Both men are Spirit-led in the way they live their lives. Both men have given their lives to the ministry of Jesus Christ. And, both men love Jesus with all of their hearts. Neither man is trying to undermine the Christian faith, nor does either man have ill-will or misaligned motivations. They simply disagree.

While their disagreement and debate is relatively civil, many Christians who follow this debate vigorously on either side have devolved into accusations and mud-slinging toward those on other side of the argument. This makes my point precisely. There is room for debate and discussion within our understanding of faith. In fact, it is absolutely essential for uncovering more truth and revelation. However, when it begins to compromise our character and identity as citizens in the Kingdom of God under the Lordship of Jesus Christ, we have monumentally missed the point. As far as I know, Jesus seemed a whole lot less concerned with everyone having every single detail nailed down and way more concerned with the heart in which each person lived out the Kingdom of God. Is this not true? The religious leaders and their followers certainly had all the right information down to every jot and tittle, but they failed to let it change their hearts for right-living.

I have a question that needs to be seriously considered. Outside of a foundational creed like the Nicene Creed, do we have to have every specific detail ironed out exactly? [46] Can we not afford each other a little bit of grace, a little bit of peace, and a little bit of patience? Can we not have different perspectives on the small things, admitting in our humility that we may not have the full revelation of God while still loving, encouraging, and building each other up? Can we not carry the burden of our brother and walk together while trying to seek and find the truth in the Spirit? The fact of the matter is that the road is too lonely to walk alone, and the battle is too tough to face on our own. We must walk together in unity.

One Kingdom

The simple fact is that this battle cannot be fought and won with little bands of resistance forces operating on their own. For this battle, it takes each one of us who call Jesus as Lord to unite behind the great proclamation and the great demonstration of the Kingdom of God to defeat the enemy. It is in the Kingdom of God that we find the one thing which unites and binds us all together and draws us out of division and denominationalism once and for all.

Do you not think if Jesus wanted to start a million and one churches and denominations He would have preached to the people about it? But we know he didn't! In fact, it is ridiculous to think that he would have. He preached *one Kingdom for all people* who follow Him. It was a call to unity, nothing less. He didn't spend His time working to make sure that every person He spoke with had an exact doctrine memorized. That wasn't His point or His purpose. His point and purpose was to initiate a Kingdom in which we would join together and walk with each other gracefully to demonstrate the ways of God on earth.

Can we break down these walls and sweep this denominational rubbish under the carpet once and for all? Seriously. Wouldn't it be great to never have to say the word denomination again? When I simply thought of that a sense of peace just ran through my entire body. Can we join together in this mighty and magnificent Kingdom of God? My God, bring us together as one in your Kingdom!

Just as a body is one but has many parts that form this one body, the same is true in Christ. We were baptized by one Spirit to form one body. We lose our individual identities and become hidden in Christ. He is the head and we are the body. His ways become our ways. His Kingdom is our Kingdom. And in His Kingdom there is no room for other kingdoms. There is no room for political kingdoms that divide. There is no room for nationalistic kingdoms that divide. There is no room for religious kingdoms that divide. And, there is certainly NO ROOM for your own individual kingdom.

There is only one Kingdom and it is to that Kingdom *we must* unite and conform! It is to that Kingdom we must pledge our allegiance. That is why it should not surprise us that the Kingdom of God is the great unifier! *Because it was the Kingdom of God that Jesus was calling us into all along.* He was calling and inviting us into His Kingdom and *only* His Kingdom. It is the Kingdom for which we have been called to take in word and action to the nations, baptizing and making disciples, so as to complete the Body of Christ. That *is* the Gospel message that we join together to proclaim! The Gospel message is nothing more and nothing less than the Gospel of the Kingdom of God! *That* is the Good News! It is for *that* Good News we share a united voice. There is no other message that is more important.

One Message

I want to talk to you about the word *Gospel* for just a moment. This may be one of the most difficult portions of this book to follow, so please take your time and follow me because I believe that understanding this word will go a long way toward bringing us together, uniting us in one voice to announce the Good News of the Kingdom of God.

The word *Gospel* comes from the Greek word *euangelion*, which means *good message*. If you look closely at that word, you will find several words that are used in the church today. The word *angel* means *messenger*. The word *evangel* is a *message which is good*. The word *evangelist* means *one who proclaims the good message or the good news*. The word *evangelization* means *the process of going out to proclaim the good news*. All of these words find their root in the word *euangelion*, which again means *good message or good news*.

The Greek word *euangelion* was used throughout the original translation of the New Testament to convey the idea of the good message, or the Good News. The angel announced *euangelion* to the shepherds in the field. John the Baptist announced *euangelion* that the Kingdom of God was near. Jesus went from town to town announcing *euangelion* of the Kingdom of God. And then, throughout the rest of the New Testament from the book of Acts through the book of Revelation the *euangelion* was preached by every single disciple and every single follower of Christ at the very risk of their death! From the very beginning of the New Testament to the very end, *euangelion* is consistently *the Good News of the Kingdom of God!*

It was when *euangelion* was translated into the King James Version that it began to lose its intended meaning. *Euangelion* was translated from Greek into the Old English word *godspel, or good tidings,* in the King

James Version. It was later rendered just *gospel,* which still meant Good News, and we began to use in our churches. As time passed, the word *Gospel* began taking on a variety of meanings by a variety of people in a variety of contexts. The original idea of the *Good News of the Kingdom of God* was lost.

As a result, the *Gospel* we have been preaching in our churches has had very little to do with the Kingdom of God, even though that was *the only Good News* everyone in the New Testament preached. Unfortunately, we have spent much of our time believing that Paul preached a different message than Jesus. We have said, "Jesus preached the Kingdom, but Paul preached the Gospel." Yet it is completely lost on us that the *Gospel* is the *Good News of the Kingdom of God!* It is one and the same thing!

Every time in the New Testament that Paul talks about the Gospel, we must understand that he is talking about *the Good News of the Kingdom of God leading up to and culminating in the death and resurrection of Christ!* It was Paul who boldly preached the Good News of the Kingdom of God and taught about the Lord Jesus Christ. We can be certain the reason Paul and the early Church were so obsessed with preaching the Good News of the Kingdom of God was because it was precisely what Jesus preached himself. Not only were the majority of the parables about the Kingdom of God, Jesus himself said that, "This *Gospel of the Kingdom* will be preached in the whole world as a testimony to all nations and then the end will come."[47] So, if we have been preaching the Gospel, or the Good News, about anything other than the Kingdom of God we *must* quit preaching it and become students, inhabitants, and preachers of this Kingdom!

There may be some of you reading who may take issue with me saying that the *Gospel* is the *Good News announcement of the Kingdom of God,* even though that is exactly what the Matthew, Mark, Luke, and John claim that Jesus preached. There are many who believe that the *Gospel* is *only* the announcement of what God has done through Jesus to reconcile sinners through the death and resurrection of Christ. In fact, this is the narrow Gospel many of our churches preach, but it is only part of the Good News.

I am not saying it is wrong to preach this feature of the Good News, but I am saying that we have not preached the full Good News of the entire Kingdom of God. *Again, our focus many times is on the individual features of the car rather than on the entire car.* It is equivalent to a car salesman who only wants to talk to every customer about the engine of the car to the neglect of the entire car. The engine is wildly important, but the customers deserve to learn about the entire car. The Kingdom of God is the larger car and of the way, the teachings, the life, the death, and the resurrection of Jesus are the individual features. The entire Kingdom of God is the Good News, not just one or two components of it.

And guess what? Paul nailed it! He absolutely nailed it! Paul understood the entirety of the Good News, not just a couple of components. It wasn't *only* a message of Christ's death and resurrection and the reconciliation of humanity to God, even though that was the crowning achievement of the Kingdom of God. Paul understood the full power of the Kingdom of God was the *entirety of the message and the embodiment of the Kingdom of God in Jesus,* which *included* the death and resurrection. The Good News of the Kingdom of God was ALL OF JESUS through and through.

Paul understood the full scope, scale, and power of the Good News of the Kingdom of God. He understood how it broke into the kingdoms of the world, how it defeated sin and death through the power of the cross and resurrection, how it freed the captives, and how it established Christ's Kingdom in the hearts and minds of his loyal subjects who gave Him their full and uncompromising allegiance!

The Good News of the Kingdom of God is the life of Christ. It is the parables of Christ. It is the teachings of Christ. It is the death of Christ. It is the resurrection of Christ. It is the defeat of sin and death by Christ. It is the rescue from the kingdoms of the world by Christ. And, it is Christ bringing everything back to Himself, including every one of us. Praise God for such Good News!

Paul understood this in such a profound way that he gave his life to proclaiming it! I absolutely love the last paragraph in the book of Acts when it says, "[Paul] lived in [Rome] two whole years at his own expense, and welcomed all who came to him, proclaiming the Kingdom of God and teaching about the Lord Jesus Christ with all boldness and without hindrance."[48]

He understood that it was more than just "saying the right words to get to heaven when you die," but rather an entirely new way of living and conducting our lives as citizens of heaven by the power of the cross, resurrection, and the gift of the Holy Spirit. Again, and I cannot emphasize this point enough: the Gospel is not simply "get saved so you can go to heaven when you die!" *The good news of the Kingdom is that Jesus broke into the kingdoms of the world in order to defeat the powers and principalities of evil so as to establish a Kingdom made of people who trust in the power of God, who are empowered by the Holy Spirit, and who look like Jesus in every facet* and pursuit of life. *The Gospel of the Kingdom is important for every person in the world right* **now**...*not just when we die!*

At this point, there should not be any confusion about the Kingdom message that we ought to be proclaiming to the world! There should not be any confusion as to the unity that the Kingdom of God calls us to put into practice. There should not be any division between Kingdom-minded people. The obvious question we must ask at this point as we look at the state of the Church is, "Why is Christ still divided?"[49] He wasn't divided in the early Church and he shouldn't be now. If it was possible then, why would it not be possible now? The Good News of the Kingdom is not only great news for the world, it is great news for the people of God who have remained fractured within denominations and individual churches for too long. But the more we distance ourselves from and fail to understand, discover, preach, and embody the Kingdom of God, the less likely we will be united. As long as we continue to preach any other Gospel than the Kingdom of God in our churches and around the world, we should continue to expect the same miserable results.

Kingdom Preached to All Nations

The singular voice announcing the Good News of the Kingdom of God to the world has been silenced. The Good News of the Kingdom of God that unites us all in one accord has been buried. The one message that the world needs to hear that will usher in the return of Jesus Christ has been lost and must be rediscovered. Yes, again, it was Jesus himself who said, "And this *Gospel of the Kingdom* will be preached in the whole world as a testimony to all nations, and then the end will come."

How can we deny the centrality of the Kingdom of God any longer? How can we deny that *this is the singular message and reality of Jesus Christ* and the reason for which He was sent? How can we claim to follow the way, life, and teachings of Jesus but not know about this Kingdom that He announced? How can we ever expect to be the united Body of Christ in the world if we continue to ignore the Kingdom of God that unites each one of us who call Jesus as Lord? How will the world ever know the Good News of the Kingdom of God if it is not proclaimed and demonstrated by us?

My Friend, part 2

You may be wondering what ever happened to my friend who was ready to discard Christianity because of the wild and erratic outburst of her mother-in-law and all the division within Christianity. That day, after she told me her story, I began to tell her about Jesus. I told her that she had to stop looking at individual Christians and churches and begin looking for Jesus and His Kingdom.

I continued on, "Jesus is calling and inviting each of us into a new reality that takes us out of the broken systems of the world and gives us a fresh breath, a new start, and a new life. Jesus is inviting us into a Kingdom that reigns in our hearts and minds, and that transforms us through the power of the Holy Spirit and into His likeness. The old ways are gone and the new ways have come. We are renewed and have become a new creation. We are just a hint of what is yet to come when all of creation is renewed through and through."

"This new way looks like loving your friend and your enemy, forgiving without end, becoming the very least and serving all of humanity, blessing those who curse you, not repaying evil with evil but evil with good. It looks like standing up for justice, standing beside those who are oppressed and extending mercy to the least of these. It is a Kingdom that starts small but breaks out into the world like a mustard seed growing wildly and completely taking over. It turns the world upside-down, destroys the works of Satan, and prepares this place for Christ's return when He will finally defeat death, put all things under His authority, and make all things new. It is into that Kingdom life that Jesus invites you."

When I finished telling her about Jesus and the Kingdom of God, she just stared at me smiling and said, "That is what I want to be a part of!" All I could say back to her was, "Of course you do. We all do. But no one has been telling us about it."

That is what the entire world wants to be a part of and has been looking for but cannot find. People are tired of religion and religious games and are hungry for life to the fullest found in the Kingdom of God. We all have a void that we have been trying to fill for so long, and we have filled it with anything and everything else that we can get our hands on except the rich treasures of the Kingdom of God.

Here is a foundational truth of life: even if we could be given all the riches of the world they would pale in comparison to the riches of the Kingdom of God. There is just nothing more beautiful. Maybe that is why the Church in all of its worldliness has become so hideous and ugly- so the world can truly see how ugly religion is and how beautiful the Kingdom of God is when it is finally revealed. It is Jesus who continues to invite you into His Kingdom that begins now and that will never end. If you haven't been able to see it before, I hope that you can see it now. The Kingdom of God is the greatest treasure that has ever been unearthed, and there are no riches in the world that will ever compare.

CHAPTER 10

WHAT WILL YOU DO WITH THIS KINGDOM?

Imagine working for a multi-billion dollar company in which the employer decided to leave the country for a year, but before leaving divided the entire company up among all the employees, giving each person responsibilities based upon his or her gifts, talents, and abilities, circle of influence, and the position held. Many of the employees were excited about the opportunity and believed it to be an honor to be asked by the employer to take on such responsibility while he was gone. To those employees having a large circle of influence and high position, much responsibility was given. These employees worked tirelessly, assumed responsibility for what they had been given, and worked to improve it and make it better because they knew that their hard work would result in greater riches for the company. But because they respected the employer so much, for he was a fair and generous man, they did not work hard to receive a reward or a portion of the riches. They worked hard for him because they were honored to work on his behalf and they wanted to do their very best.

At the same time, there were other workers whom the employer thought very highly of as well. He hired them because they were eager to work for him. To these workers the employer gave responsibilities that had the potential to make the company a lot of money. In fact, the employer believed that if these employees were wise and if they worked hard, they could actually double the earnings for the company in the areas for which they had been given responsibility. While their responsibilities were not perceived as important as those of the first workers, there was still a lot of responsibility in their work and a lot of potential to grow the business. Their work was just as important to the overall performance of the business as the first workers, and they were just as eager to make the company successful for the employer.

To make sure that all of the employees had a share in the responsibility for the company while he was gone, the employer met with the rest of the employees and gave them the final share. There was no way that the company could continue to function, make money, and be successful unless every single employee took a part of that which was given to him and worked hard to produce more. This was especially true for this final group of employees. While it was true the employer had given them the smallest share of responsibility, he believed it was possible for the employees to use their gifts, talents, and abilities along with hard work to increase the company's bottom-line.

After the employer had been gone on his travels for quite some time, he sent a memo throughout the company indicating that he would soon be returning and that he would like to have a company-wide banquet in honor of his return. He also indicated that he would like to meet with each division of employees separately before the banquet in order to share their performance results and disclose the percentage by which they were able to grow the business while he had been gone. The anticipation of the employer's return was growing and preparations were being made for a great banquet. The owner made specific requests for the finest meats and the choicest wines to line the tables upon his return.

When the owner finally made his appearance after being gone for so long, the employees lined the entryway. The cheering and applause were deafening as this fine and well-respected man made his way down the red carpet that the employees had laid out in his honor. As he walked by the employees he shook their hands and gave them hugs as he gradually made his way into the meeting room.

The employer took a few minutes to get settled in at his table, and after he laid out his employee progress notes he called for the first group. The mood was still quite festive with cheers and shouts still coming from outside as the first group of employees filled the room. Without having to be asked, the group reported that over the last year they doubled the company's projections and smashed their goal for the year. Elated, the employer declared that with results like this he should stay away more often. Each employee was praised and told by the employer that he or she would receive a promotion with more responsibility for their fine work. Because they had proven that they could be trusted with what he had given them, they could now be trusted with more.

Much to the surprise and the excitement of the employer, the second group of employees shared that they had also doubled the company's annual projections. This group of employees was a lot more rowdy than the first group. They were hollerin' and shoutin' and giving each other high-fives. The employer couldn't do anything but laugh at the level of excitement that this group displayed. As a result of their top-notch and much better than expected results, the employer announced to the employees that he was going to give them all promotions as well and increase their level of responsibility within the company.

As they left the room, they were still clappin' and shoutin', giving the final group of employees "bro hugs" on their way out of the meeting room. The room soon emptied and was quickly filling again, this time with the final group of employees. They were in good spirits as they circled around the table, all still smiling, drunk off of the excitement that had been spilling out of the room. The employer himself was standing and clapping, grinning from ear to ear as a proud parent would be at the good work of his children. He slowly made his way back to his seat and settled in for the final report.

"Sir, we would like to report that over the last year we did not lose any money. In fact, we maintained exactly what you gave us responsibility for."

Puzzled, the employer looked at the employees and asked them to repeat what they just reported.

"Sir, you heard us correctly. We decided that it would not be wise to disturb the work you gave us to do. It would have been too risky. Everything was working fine the way it was, so we decided not to mess it up. We were concerned that if we messed it up you would be mad at us."

"Let me get this straight. You thought that I would be mad at you, so you didn't do anything at all to grow the company while I was gone! Are you fools? Look at the gifts, talents, and abilities that you have! Look at the ingenuity and creativity that you have among you! And with all of the giftedness that you have, you spent the last year squandering countless opportunities to just maintain the business! I would have been better off taking the money I invested in you and just sticking it in the bank! That way I would have at least earned some interest on it!"

If there was a spirit of festivity earlier, there was not a trace of it now. The hollerin' and shoutin' had long since passed, and now the only thing that could be heard was the fidgeting of the employees in the conference room.

The fidgeting was soon overpowered by the deep, stern voice of the employer when he announced to the employees that they were all fired and that their responsibilities would be handed over to the first group of employees who had proven they could be responsible for what they had been given.

"But sir, we thought that you would be proud of us for maintaining the business!"

"The employees who take responsibility for what I give them, who use every resource I provide them, and who use their unique talents and abilities to make this company row are the employees to whom I will always give more responsibility. As for you, because you squandered your responsibility, ignored the resources I made available to you, and wasted all of your talent and ability, everything has been taken from you today."[50]

What Will You Do With This Kingdom?

What will you do with the responsibility and the task you have been given? The employer left each of us in charge of his multi-billion dollar company and divided up the responsibility accordingly. Are you working hard for the generous employer, not because of some reward that you will receive, but because your respect and gratitude toward the employer propels you into action? Are you using all of the resources that the employer has so generously left for you to make him proud of the work you have done? Are you using the unique gifts, talents, and abilities you have been given to beautifully, creatively, and lovingly grow the Kingdom of God in the world? Or, are you content with squandering the opportunity that you have been given?

We have been given such an awesome task and responsibility by the Creator of the universe. We have been given every resource that we need at our disposal. We have been given the most diverse and unique talents, gifts, and abilities for the task at hand. We have been given a portion of the great responsibility of spreading, sharing, and growing the Kingdom of God. But what will you do with this Kingdom? I will ask it again, *what will you do with this Kingdom*?

If you had previously never heard of this Kingdom until now, will you turn away from the dead-end pursuits of the world? Will you turn from your agnosticism, atheism, and universalism to join the Kingdom movement that is lifting people up, healing the broken-hearted, drawing people together, and extending love, forgiveness, justice, and mercy to every person in the world? Will you leave your indifference and apathy to join this non-religious movement behind the way and life of Jesus? Will you awaken from the dead in order to be a revolutionary who will also wake the sleepwalkers who are among you? This is the place where life and fulfillment are found- only in the Kingdom of God.

If you are in the Church and find yourself in a religious system, will you break the shackles that have been binding you in order to find the freedom that is in the Kingdom of God? Will you stay locked in the religious system or will you share in the great riches of the Kingdom of God? Will you share these riches of the Kingdom of God with your brothers and sisters within your churches who have never heard of this Kingdom and who are locked into religious, superficial, or inward pursuits themselves? Will you take these riches of the Kingdom of God that you have found and share them with other people in your communities and around the world? Will you be the one who is the Kingdom catalyst with your pastors, elders, and other church leadership? Will you be the mighty clarion call of the Kingdom of God proclaiming unity for every follower of Christ within your community? To whom much is given, much is expected, and the great riches of the Kingdom have now been given to you. What will you do with them?

Bottom Up

If the Kingdom of God is truly like the mustard seed, it starts small and grows from the bottom up and then outward and onward. The Kingdom of God happens at the grassroots level, and that means it starts with you! Remember, Jesus did not try to reform the religious institution, or the world from the top down. Rather he went to the common man and common woman and started the Kingdom revolution at the very bottom. The Kingdom of God movement is not about one man or one woman leading this revolution. It is not about churches of people waiting for their leadership or denominations to figure it out and lead the Kingdom march. It begins *now* and it begins with *you and others at the bottom* mobilizing to *be the change in your churches and in your communities.* Our churches will only change when we begin to change ourselves. Our churches will only begin to be the means through which the Kingdom of God extends into the world when *we* stop making our centralized churches the end-all-be-all. The Church is the people…and we are the means through which the Kingdom of God extends out into the world.

Let it be known that we, as those who embody the Kingdom of God, are the salt of the earth that bring out the rich flavors of life so the entire world can taste and see how good the Lord is![51] We are the light of the world, a light that has been put on a stand in the house, shining bright for the entire world to see our good deeds so that they may glorify our Father in heaven![52] We are the seeds of wheat that are growing among the weeds in the fields of the world![53] We are the mustard seeds that have been sown and that grow upward and outward overtaking everything in our path to spread the Kingdom of God! We are the yeast in the dough of the world that is worked through and through until the Kingdom of God is in all and through all! We are the in-breaking Kingdom of God that goes out into every part of the world, in every situation, every circumstance, and every relationship and tells every man, woman, and child that Jesus is Lord and his Kingdom has come! We put this Kingdom on display tirelessly through our lives, extending it with every breath that we take and with every single heartbeat.

The great treasure of the Kingdom of God has been opened, and you have been given the riches. Again I ask, "What will you do with that which you have been given and that for which you are responsible?" Will you hold on to the riches for yourself, or share them with the world? We are those who have been called to *go* into the world, to *go* into all the nations, and to spread the Good News of the Kingdom, calling the world to discipleship and completing the Body of Christ.

Movement

It means movement. It means action. It means progression. We have to *go* into the world! We cannot wait for the world to come to us! We have been called to be in the world even though we are not of the world. We have been called to preach and live out the Kingdom of God outside of our church buildings and in the homes and neighborhoods throughout our communities so as to enjoy the favor of the people around us. We have been called to sit among the sinners, the prostitutes, the tax-collectors of our world to announce that there is a new Kingdom in town, and it is going to turn not only their lives but the entire created order upside-down! But we have to put one foot in front of the other and march out from behind the walls of our churches where we have been hiding. We have to be willing to move away from the comfort and benefits of our churches and learn to be the self-sacrificial Church together in the neighborhoods and streets of the world.

We are the Body of Christ. We are the transformed. We are the voices preaching the Good News. We are the hands caring for the elderly, giving food to the hungry, and lifting up the downtrodden. We are the mouths and voices that encourage the single mother, praise the fatherless child, and pray for the broken-hearted. We are the feet standing beside the oppressed, walking with the lonely, and running into the neighborhoods meeting every person in their places of pain. We are the means through which God puts back together that which has been broken, finds that which has been lost, and picks up that which has been cast aside.

As you look around your neighborhoods and your communities, is it not obvious that it is the sick who need a doctor, not the healthy?[54] Is it not obvious that we have been called to humble ourselves and reach out to the sinners and the least in the world in love and grace, not just to stand among and call on the righteous? Is it not obvious by now that the harvest of the world is so great, but the workers are so few?[55] Who among us will accept this Kingdom and answer the Lord and say, "Here am I, send me!"[56] Send me among the nations to spread this Kingdom! Send me into the villages, the neighborhoods, the projects, the apartments, the slums, the barrios, the prisons, and the gutters of the world! Send me to be a living, breathing conduit of your peace, grace, justice, mercy, forgiveness, and love in every dark corner of creation! Send me to be but a sheep among the wolves for your Kingdom and your Kingdom purposes in the world![57]

A Prayerful Call to the Church

But God, give us the eyes to see the world as you see it! Give us the ears to hear and understand the gentle whisper of your Spirit! Give us a heart and give us a voice to tell the world about your Kingdom! Give us the courage to stand tall in gentleness and love before every man and every woman, from our friends to the mighty governing authorities, and give us the words that you would have us say at just the right time! Let our lives be an out-breaking of your eternal power and your divine nature in such a miraculous and remarkable way that it is nothing but a clear and understandable demonstration of your Kingdom and your reign throughout the land!

Let us fight the good fight against the powers and principalities of evil and not against our brothers and sisters in the world, and certainly not against our brothers and sisters within the Church. Let us march forward in the power of the Spirit, offering sight to the blind, giving freedom to the enslaved, and announcing to the world that their debts have been cancelled, their sins have been forgiven, and their lives and their land have been reclaimed because of the victory of Jesus Christ! Let us follow courageously behind the only Lord who will never be defeated, for even the greatest enemy that stood against His Kingdom has been defeated by the power of self-sacrificial love demonstrated on a cross and by the conquering of death through resurrection. Let us be a demonstration to the world of the same kind of self-sacrificial love that was demonstrated and expressed through Jesus Christ.

Let us declare with our mouths to the nations that the Kingdom of God has come, is turning over the empty ways of the world, and is offering hope and life to the fullest. Let us declare with our lives that heaven and earth are becoming one as we testify to how the Lord is making all things new, even in us. Let us stand together in unity so the world will know once and for all that Jesus is Lord over all of His good creation and that His love abounds for each and every man, woman, and child. Let us extend a Kingdom that reigns in peace and justice, forgiveness and mercy, reconciliation and unity, and above all, humble and self-sacrificial love. It is only through this kind of testimony and demonstration of the Gospel of the Kingdom of God to all the nations that the end of the Age will come.

Let us put our faith, hope, trust, and allegiance in a Kingdom that will last and will not be destroyed. While all of the worlds systems are beginning to shake violently, while all of the world's economies are set upon foundations that are as sturdy as sand, and while all of the world's governments are falling like mighty towers, let us receive a Kingdom that cannot be shaken! When the governments of the world begin to crumble, let us have the Kingdom of God! When the political leaders of this world continue to fail us, let us have the Kingdom of God! When every single ideology and pursuit and wisdom of man fails, and they will, let us have the Kingdom of God! For our God is a mighty consuming fire, and while every single thing not of heaven will be shaken, His Kingdom will continue to endure forever and forever.

Let us stand united shoulder to shoulder in the wedding hall in great anticipation of what is to come. Let us gather together and await the opening of the doors that will welcome us in to the celebration of the Ages. Let us take off our old and tired rags that are soiled with the muck and mire of days past and put on the wedding clothes of righteousness so as to be appropriately dressed for such an occasion. Let us clothe ourselves in the righteous acts of the saints for we know that our labor in the Lord has not been done in vain and will not be wasted.[58]

For the riches of this mighty treasure that were once hidden deep within the ground have been revealed and are now being shared for the renewing of the world, and the power of this treasure is extending into the hearts and minds of every man, woman, and child, transforming every relationship, situation, and circumstance through and through. Father God, let us proclaim with our mouths and our lives, and in unison with the Holy Spirit, "Your Kingdom come, Your will be done, on earth as it is in heaven."[59]

The Anticipation

The marriage of the Bride and the Bridegroom is imminent and that which has been separated will finally be united together forever. For up until this time, all of creation has been groaning and awaiting liberation from the bondage to death and decay so as to be brought into the freedom and glory of the children of God. We stand in eager anticipation as the doors will one day open wide and we will join the four living creatures, the twenty-four elders, thousands upon thousands of angels, and the entire created order to sing a new song together:

> Worthy is the Lamb, who was slain,
> to receive power and wealth and wisdom and strength
> and honor and glory and praise!

> To him who sits on the throne and to the Lamb
> be praise and honor and glory and power,
> for ever and ever! Revelation 5: 12-13 (edited)

For this Jesus is the image of the invisible God, the firstborn over all of creation. And by Him *all things* were created: things in heaven and on earth, visible and invisible, whether thrones or powers or rulers or authorities; all things were created by Him and for Him. He is before all things, and in Him all things hold together.

And He is the head of the body, the Church. He is the beginning and the firstborn from among the dead, *so that in everything He might have the supremacy.* For God was pleased to have all His fullness dwell in Him, and *through Him to reconcile to himself all things,* whether things on earth or things in heaven, by making peace through his blood, shed on the cross.[60]

Since death came through a man, the resurrection of the dead comes also through a man. As in Adam all die, so in Christ all will be made alive. But each in his own turn: Christ, the first fruits; then, when He comes, those who belong to Him. Then the end will come, when He hands over the Kingdom to God the Father after He has destroyed all dominion, authority and power. He must reign until He has put all His enemies under his feet. The last enemy to be destroyed is death. He "has put everything under His feet." When He has done this, then the Son Himself will be made subject to the Father who put everything under Him, *so that God may be all in all.*[61] And then the kingdoms of the world will become the Kingdom of our Lord and of His Christ, and He will reign for ever and ever. Amen and amen.[62]

CHAPTER 11

THE DAILY KINGDOM

I love the outdoors. Any chance I get to hop on a trail…I take it. Each year I, along with some of my close guy friends, plan a hiking and canoeing trip somewhere in the United States. The hikes we usually take involve some relatively significant elevation changes that push the limits of our- ok, *my* endurance.

During many of the long, grueling ascents, I can be heard yelling out to the group at the top of my lungs, "Where's the payoff?! Where's the payoff?!" I usually get some laughs and some general agreement because they all know that while the ascent is quite a bit of work and very draining, there is usually a big "payoff" for the heavy-legged hikers. At the top, or just around the bend, there is the most magnificent vista overlooking an expansive valley and mighty river. It is breath-taking. All of the work that it took to get to that point was worth it. It was *well worth it!*

This book may have taken some time, energy, and effort on your part to work through. In fact, I could almost hear you saying, "Where's the payoff?! Where's the payoff?!" It is my hope that we have rounded the bend, reached the top, and now are coming close to appreciating the magnificent vista that overlooks the beauty that lies ahead. It is a view of the daily Kingdom lived out in our lives, our relationships, and in our church communities. This is the "payoff" and the view for which we have all been waiting to see revealed.

Full Disclosure

Through this entire project, I have only wanted God to use me to open your eyes and to change your hearts and your minds toward the Kingdom of God. With everything in me, and with fervent prayers on my knees, I am praying for you and for the Church to rise from what we have settled for and into what we have always been destined to become. I have not poured my heart and soul into this project in order to have people who already agree with me continue to nod their heads in more agreement that the walls are torn down and are in desperate need of repair.

I want to reiterate something that I stated at the beginning of this project. I am pouring my heart and soul out: to those of you who have not realized until now how broken, dysfunctional, and misaligned we are as a group of people who proclaim to follow Christ, to those of you who have not known what the Kingdom of God is, and to those of you who have not realized that the Kingdom of God is the identity and purpose of the Church, to those of you who have perpetuated a religious system, willingly or unwillingly, to those of you who hold on tightly to power, control, and politics within your churches, to those of you who have commercialized Jesus and your churches in order to attract and entertain people who are hungry to consume, to those of you who have been living inside of the torn down and devastated walls and who have been there for so long you don't even noticed the problems. I beg of you, please- have the eyes to see the problems. Honestly look at yourself and your church as you read the following pages. Let the Truth of Christ pierce your heart and awaken your Spirit to the way of Jesus and His Kingdom in your life and in the life of your church.

My spiritual mentor, whom I love dearly, was a pastor of an old country church in the middle of Indiana. He is someone who loves, lives, and embodies the Kingdom of God with as much sincerity and fervor as anyone as I have ever seen. He took on this particular ministry position as an opportunity to walk beside and help a dying church find its life and identity in the Kingdom of God that it had been missing.

It had not been much over a year before a select few began waging the power and politics game in his church, pushing for him to be fired. For what, you may ask? Nothing more than preaching Jesus and His Kingdom and asking for sacrifice and unity from all who want to follow Christ. The day before the elders caved in to the political pressure and fired him, he sent me this message:

What I am going through right now is proof positive that the Church, as an institution, is beyond repair. It is a broken system. The "keepers of the system" will not hear from "on high" as Scripture predicates. Their system favors keeping a totalitarian control on their institution. For example, if the system does not like their pastor's teaching, they do all the usual things: name smearing, withholding tithes, pressure to quit. If that fails, they demand a congregational vote whose rules have been drawn up to favor their system and status quo. Like our government, it is a system that is broken. Putting better men and women into that system will not fix it, rather it just destroys them. They too soon adopt the tactics of the system (in theory to defeat it), yet they in fact perpetuate it.

Ask yourself where you and your church have missed the Kingdom way of life, and then get down on your knees in repentance. Ask God to change your hearts and minds. This is not how the Kingdom of God operates! God forgive us! Ask, plead, and beg God to give you the *courage* in leading those around you, especially those in your church. Pray for the people around you to begin seeing the issues, so that you may all begin rebuilding and repairing the devastated walls together. Pray that God would give you protection from those who try to hold on to the ways and workings of the world in your church and those who try to disrupt this Kingdom rebuilding. Pray that God will either change their hearts and minds so that they may work for the rebuilding of His Kingdom within your church, or that they will part ways so as to not be a disruption to this important work.

As we move forward prayerfully, ask yourself what role will you play in this rebuilding. *Everyone* is needed and *everyone* has role. Are you the person who will gather together others to begin rebuilding? Are you the person who will work with others to see the problem and then begins to lay out the plans for change? Are you the one who will lead and sing praises to God for the work that is being done? Are you the person who will encourage those who are instrumental in the rebuilding? Are you the person who will pray, not just for the rebuilding but for protection from those who will try to disrupt this important Kingdom work? Are you the person who will teach the children of your church about the Kingdom of God and then leads them into the great rebuilding? Are you the person who will continue to ask yourself and others the question, "What is keeping our church from looking like the Kingdom of God in everything we do?" The truth is that God, in mighty and miraculous ways, will use each of you who are committed to bringing His Kingdom to life within your lives and churches. Let the rebuilding begin.

From Theology to Practice

A Kingdom life is the victory of God, the exaltation of God in flesh through Jesus Christ, and the power of the Holy Spirit working in and through faithful followers of Christ in every situation and circumstance, from the very best to the very worst, in order to extend God's reign on earth as it is in heaven. As a Church, we are the embodiment of what it looks like for the full reign of God to work in and through our lives so that the whole world will be drawn to Jesus Christ as Lord and to His Kingdom.

As lofty and high-arching as this sounds, it has very real implications for both the follower of Christ, and then as a result, the Church. As the individual goes, so goes the Church…because we *are* the Church. As we change as individuals, the Church will necessarily change as well. When we give ourselves over to the reign of God in our individual lives, we then become Christ to the world as the Church. As a result, it is essential to discuss how the Kingdom of God transforms both- the individual and then naturally, the Church.

So if the Church has become misaligned in any way, shape, or form from what it looks like to embody the Kingdom of God on earth as it is in heaven then it is a necessary for each one of us to be transformed. It is imperative for the lives of followers of Christ, and then subsequently for the life and purpose of the Church, that we discover the practical life application of the Kingdom of God. We must discover what the Kingdom life looks like lived daily and how it differs from our current form of "churchianity." While it is impossible to describe and list out every single example of how the Kingdom of God transforms and changes every single part of a person, and then how those things then change the Church, let this chapter serve as a snapshot of the heart and soul of the Kingdom in practice, revealing how it may begin to transform us from what we have been into what we need to become.

Jesus Christ Alone

Our beginning and focal point must be Jesus Christ. The crowning achievement of God is Jesus Christ defeating sin and death so as to pull heaven and earth back together under one head, initiating His reconciliation plan through humanity who has submitted to His way and His Kingdom. The celebration of the Ages looks centrally at Jesus Christ and the reestablishment of God's rule and God's reign throughout the entire cosmos. The towering pinnacle of the Ages is Jesus Christ breaking into the rogue kingdoms of the world and establishing a Kingdom to be the face of God's love and righteousness in the world. It is in Jesus that the full reign and accomplishment of God centers and extends. God was pleased to have his very fullness dwell in Christ so that he might have reign and supremacy in all and through all.

> [Christ] is the image of the invisible God, the firstborn over all creation. For by him all things were created: things in heaven and on earth, visible and invisible, whether thrones or powers or rulers or authorities; all things were created by him and for him. He is before all things, and in him all things hold together. And he is the head of the body, the church; he is the beginning and the firstborn from among the dead, so that in everything he might have the supremacy. For God was pleased to have all his fullness dwell in him, and through him to reconcile to himself all things, whether things on earth or things in heaven, by making peace through his blood, shed on the cross. Colossians 1: 15-20

> And he made known to us the mystery of his will according to his good pleasure, which he purposed in Christ, to be put into effect when the times will have reached their fulfillment—to bring all things in heaven and on earth together under one head, even Christ. Ephesians 1: 9-10

It is under the headship of Jesus Christ where we find the Body of Christ, the Church, the people who embody the union of heaven and earth, the people who are the first fruits of new creation, the people who are the first part of what is yet to be revealed. Christ, the Head, directs the workings of the Body. It is through Jesus Christ that the Church finds its purpose and fulfillment. It is through Jesus Christ that the Church moves in righteousness and holiness.

This is the magnificent accomplishment of God- that through Jesus He would finally have a people of His name and a people of His way. It is under the Lordship of King Jesus that a Kingdom of loyal subjects has been established to extend His rule and reign throughout the world in righteousness and mercy in order to demonstrate and then to disciple others into this life of fullness and abundance. The infusion of and the connection to Jesus is the Life-giving exclamation to humanity that there is victory in the best and highest ways of God.

We, as individuals and collectively, have become sorely disconnected from Jesus, and we have lost knowledge and awareness of His Kingdom. We have been walking in utter darkness with only glimpses of the light of Christ to direct our ways. We are hardly an entity that embodies the supremacy and majesty of God incarnate as a visible representation of Jesus Christ to the world. We have become incredibly passé and casual in our understanding of and our surrender to the might, power, and profundity of the God-man, Jesus Christ, and His in-breaking Kingdom. Our awe of the cosmic Christ who has reconciled the entire cosmos, including precious humanity, is significantly lacking and has been replaced by a very casual "Jesus is my bro" attitude. Yes, Jesus is incredibly relatable on a personal level, but we are grievously lacking in a high Christology in which Jesus is the supreme centerpiece and masterpiece of God's accomplishment to whom we give our love, our lives, and our all.

In the book *Jesus Manifesto*, Leonard Sweet and Franklin Viola capture the high Christology that is absent within the Church and the power that is available to us from on high.

The mystery of God is this…

That the One who is the visible image of the invisible God;
The One in whom all the fullness of the Godhead dwells;
The One who is the living essence of the Trinity;
The One in whom eternity lives, breathes, and has its being;
The One who is before time;
The A to Z, the Alpha and Omega, the beginning and the end;
The Firstborn of the created universe, who rose from the dead never to die again;
The Conqueror of death, sin, and the grave;
The Creator, Savior, Redeemer, and Forgiver;
The One who holds all creation together in Himself;
The One who is the power of glory and might;
The Head, the authority, and source of the Church;
The One through whom and for whom all things were created;
The One in whom all things find their meaning and reality;
The One who reconciled all things in heaven and earth to God;

The One who nailed to His bloody cross every law, every rule, every
regulation that would condemn the beloved people of God;
The One who is supreme in every realm and hold the first place in
all things- the Son of the Father's love;
The One whose significance is unmatched in human history;
The One who hold the title deed to the universe…

This glorious, limitless, amazing, incredible, expansive, incomparable,
marvelous, stunning, staggering, majestic, mighty, matchless,
spectacular, outstanding, tremendous, immense, infinite, vast,
grand, triumphant, victorious, precious, radiant, peerless, wonderful,
magnificent Christ has chosen to place all of His fullness where?
INSIDE OF YOU![63]

No one person or thing is as Life-Giving as Jesus Christ. The very
fullness of Christ in our individual lives and in the life of the Church is
all we need, nothing more. Yet we have weakened and cheapened- and in
some instances removed- Christ in such staggering proportions that we are
left longing for something that will fill us. It is no wonder that there is so
much sickness within the individual Christian and within the Church. We
have replaced that which is Life-giving with gimmicks, fads, and styles. We
operate as if we have to "compete" with our culture and our society for the
attention of the people. Jesus is sufficient and does not need to be dressed
or hyped up. He does not need a marketing campaign, slick advertising,
or demographic studies in our churches. Reread the excerpt from *The
Jesus Manifesto* above. Does it sound like Jesus needs bells and whistles
to completely capture the imagination and blow the mind of every man,
woman, and child? No, he doesn't.

We are guilty not just of trying to dress up and sell Jesus to people,
but of neglecting to simply present this mind-blowing and world altering
Christ! God forgive us. We are left longing for something, and many times
we are not even sure what it is. We become "church shoppers" and "church
hoppers" looking for something that will make us happy or fill the hole in
our lives. After the "honeymoon period" is over in one church, we are off
to another. Whenever the buzz wears off of the glitz and the glam, or when
we figure out that these people are sinful and jacked up, it is time for a new
buzz and a new group of people to hang out with. Our error in thinking is
that we believe the next group of people will not fail us or hurt us.

Can we not see the sickness in what we are doing? Can we not see how misaligned we have become in our priorities? Can we not see how consumerist- and non-Christ centered- we have become. Can we not see how our churches have continued to perpetuate the consumerist sickness by offering a smorgasbord of *everything* while watering down, and in some instances losing, Jesus? We so desperately need Jesus and Jesus alone, presented in all of His mind-blowing, mind-altering, awe-inspiring richness and fullness. We have become so misguided and misaligned in our attempts to fill the hole with unfulfilling junk, we have missed the most important and Life-giving thing.

It is only when we, as individuals and as the Church, finally figure out that style, preference, and gimmicks need to die within our houses of worship that Jesus can once again stand alone in majesty and supremacy and take center stage for the filling of His people. When we finally figure this out we will begin to change the consumer mentality within our churches and the petty arguments between generations about the style of music and the types of clothes that we wear at church on Sunday. Our preferential interests will be eclipsed by a Christ-centered awe and celebration that we, as sinners, can finally come together under His Lordship in one accord. It is when we hunger for Christ and His Kingdom alone that we will change.

We will be a people enveloped by Christ in every pursuit. Christ in our prayers. Christ in our worship. Christ in our psalms. Christ in the Lord's Supper. Christ in our baptism. Christ in our fellowship. Christ in our solitude. Christ in our silence. Christ in our words. Christ in our testimony. Christ in our blessings. Christ as we rise. Christ when we work. Christ when we eat. Christ when we play. Christ when we sleep. This is the union of the believers to Christ in all we do.

When we join together in fellowship, Christ is the centerpiece. When we lift up our praises and exalt the victory of Jesus over Satan, the kingdoms of the world, and sin and death, Christ is the centerpiece. When we stand together and speak the Psalms in one accord as our prayers with Christ, Christ is the centerpiece. When we join around the table to commemorate the body of Christ broken and the blood of Christ spilled for the forgiveness of sins, Christ is the centerpiece. When we hear the Good News of the Kingdom of God proclaimed and preached, Christ is the centerpiece. When testimony is given, declaring that the Lord brought us out of slavery and bondage and into the freedom and riches of His glorious Kingdom, Christ is the centerpiece.

When we finally put Jesus back at the center of our lives, worship, teaching, preaching, prayer and testimony, the petty bickering, complaining, "church shopping," and "church hopping" will cease, because we will have finally been confronted by, and will have found fulfillment in, Christ alone. When Christ, His ways, His teachings, and His Kingdom are made the centerpiece once again, we will be united in our churches with our brothers and sisters in Christ. The truth is that we belong to one another through the only thing that holds us together…the only thing we need. And what an enormously tight union we find in Jesus Christ and His Kingdom!

This is incredibly important in our churches, as we have carelessly given our allegiance to other kings and other kingdoms that have left us divided and in shambles. For the sake of the Kingdom of God, and for the love of the accomplishment, rule, and reign of Jesus, *brothers and sisters- pledge and declare your allegiance to Jesus Christ alone.* Be *only* His people, no matter the cost!

I was struck by a declaration that was written by George Barna in his book entitled *Revolution*. I believe that this declaration captures the heart and the Spirit to which God calls each of us through Jesus Christ as the embodiment of His Kingdom. I also believe it increases our awareness of those things we have considered important, but that have inhibited us in the past from perfect love and unity within the Church. Let this declaration be our heart's cry. Let this declaration be the anthem by which we sing and shout aloud. Let this declaration be the call of sacrifice for each follower of Christ through whom the Spirit will break the Kingdom of God out into the world.

> I am a sinner, broken by my disobedience but restored by Jesus Christ in order to participate in good works that please God. I am not perfect, but Jesus Christ makes me righteous in God's eyes, and the Holy Spirit leads me towards greater holiness. God created me for His purposes. My desire as a Revolutionary is to fulfill those ends, and those ends alone. When I get out of bed each day, I do so for one purpose: to love, obey, and serve God and His people.

> Every breath I take is a declaration of war against Satan and a commitment to opposing him. God does not need me to fight His fight, but he invites me to allow Him to fight through me. It is my privilege to serve Him in that manner. I anticipate and will gladly endure various hardships as I serve God; for this is the price of participation in winning the spiritual war.

I do not need to save the world. Jesus Christ has already done that. I cannot transform the world, but I can allow God to use me to transform some part of it. My commitment to the Revolution of faith is sealed by my complete surrender to God's ways and His will. I will gratefully do what He asks of me simply because He loves me enough to ask. I gain my security, success, and significance through my surrender to Him.

Worship is not an event I attend or a process I observe; it is the lifestyle I lead. I do not give away 10 percent of my resource. I surrender 100 percent. God has given me natural abilities and supernatural abilities, all intended to advance His Kingdom. I will deploy those abilities for that purpose.

The proof of my status as a Revolutionary is the love I show to God and people. There is strength in relationships; I am bound at a heart and soul level to other Revolutionaries, and I will bless believers whenever I have the chance. To achieve victory in the spiritual war in which we are immersed, there is nothing I must accomplish; I must simply follow Christ with everything I have. There is no greater calling than to know and serve God. The world is desperately seeking meaning and purpose. I will respond to that need with the Good News and meaningful service.

Absolute moral and spiritual truth exists, is knowable, and is intended for my life; it is accessible through the Bible. I want nothing more than to hear God say to me, "Well done, My good and faithful servant."

Thank you Lord God for loving me, for saving me, for refining me, and for including me in the work of Your Kingdom. My life is Yours to use as You please. I love you.[64]

Power From on High

We are mistaken if we believe that we have the power to do this on our own. It is not in our own power that we begin to see clearly or begin to be transformed from such superficiality and pettiness and into a Christ-centered, united Kingdom. This power must come from above. As unspectacular as we are as the Church, God gives us His power through the Holy Spirit to move and act according to the mind of Christ. It is when we have made Christ the center of our lives, and then subsequently the center of the Church, that we will receive this power from on high.

His ways will become our ways and the ways of the Church. His thoughts will become the thoughts of the Church. His actions will become the actions of the Church. His concerns will become the concerns of the Church. His love will become the love of the Church. The Church is rescued from the divided, fractured, and conditional ways of the world so as to be the whole, healed, and risen Body of Christ filled with God's power in the Holy Spirit. It is *only* through the power of the Holy Spirit that each of us can even begin to see clearly and begin to look like Jesus in everything that we do so as to be made into a Kingdom worthy of His name and a testimony to the nations.

In his book, *Power from on High*, Charles Finney writes:

> You will receive power. This was and is a unique divine inspiration, an endowment of supernatural energy affecting every department of the believer's life and remaining with him forever. It is not physical power or even mental power though it may touch everything both mental and physical in its benign outworking. It is, too, another kind of power than that seen in nature, in the lunar attraction that creates the tides or the angry flash that splits the great oak during a storm. This power from God operates on another level and affects another department of his wide creation. It is spiritual power. It is the kind of power that God is. It is the ability to achieve spiritual and moral ends. Its long-range result is to produce Godlike character in men and women who were once wholly evil by nature and by choice.

> I think there can be no doubt that the need above all other needs in the Church of God at this moment is the power of the Holy Spirit. More education, better organization, finer equipment, more advanced methods- all are unavailing. It is like bringing

a better respirator after the patient is dead. Good as these are… they can never give life. [65]

It is only through the spiritual power of the Spirit of God, and not of us, where we find that kind of Life. It is a Life in which the old sinful person dies and this new Life continues to resurrect in us and through us. It is only through the perfect example of Christ and by the leading of the Holy Spirit that we will find and know who it is we are, how we ought to be, and what it is we ought to pursue. The Spirit gives us a new heart and a new mind, teaching us in the ways of grace, mercy, love, and unity with our brothers and sisters. While it is true that Jesus Christ is the one we have decorated, stylized, hyped up, or even pushed to the backburner, it is the power of the Holy Spirit we have ignored and grieved. The very power of God that unites us and teaches us how to live as citizens in the Kingdom of God has been painfully cut off and we are paying the price for it.

Without submission to the power of the Holy Spirit in our lives, our relationships, and in our churches, we will be in conflict- and we have been. The spirit by which we have operated is a spirit of selfishness. We continually think about what we can get out of something, what meets our preferences, or what accommodates us rather than what we can give or what is best for the Kingdom. We all know "It's not about me," but do we even think about practicing it? Do we consider what it might look like lived out daily in our lives? Do we take the Spirit of selflessness with us in our relationships with others, including our marriages and friendships? Do we take the Spirit of selflessness with us into our churches? If not, then why? What power exactly do we trust in…the power of the Holy Spirit or our own? I think we all know the answer, but who is confronting us with this Truth?

I know people who protest the style of praise music that we sing in our church, and as a result, they do not sing to God. Do we not recognize that our words of praise may not be for God alone, but for the person standing right next to us who needs to hear those words of assurance and healing? By withholding our praise because of our selfish protest, we are not simply neglecting our praise of God, we are refusing to be a means through which God ministers to others. In the ways of the kingdoms of the world, we protest and refuse to participate in something if it is not done to our liking. In the Kingdom of God, we practice the presence of God in every single aspect of life, the good and the bad, giving praise to God with every breath we take while realizing that our lives are not our own.

I know people who neglect to meet weekly with their brothers and sisters in Christ because they do not think they will get anything out of it. We have made our gatherings about ourselves and what we can get out of it rather than the celebration of God and the ministry opportunity of breathing life and love into our brothers and sisters whom we have the pleasure to edify and serve. This kind of selfishness is not of God and there is no room in the Kingdom of God for such selfishness. In the ways of the kingdoms of the world, we determine what we do or what we participate in by what we can get out of it. In the Kingdom of God we find the greatest honor and pleasure on earth in gathering together with our brothers and sisters in Christ, always looking for the opportunity to serve, *not* to be served ourselves. In the Kingdom of God it is never about what we get out of something, but what the Spirit of God can give through us as we humble ourselves in service.

I know married couples who have proclaimed Christ with their lips, yet live lives that are so selfish and self-focused that their marriage ends in separation or divorce. It is in our relationships with others, especially in our marriages, that we have ignored the leading of the Spirit and instead forged our own selfish way. The ways of the kingdoms of the world teach us to harbor anger, frustration, and impatience, while choosing the way of resentment and non-forgiveness. In the Kingdom of God, the Spirit of God unites, mends, heals, and brings back together that which is fractured, divided, and broken, and teaches us the way of selflessness, forgiveness, and reconciliation with everyone. When anything opposes mending, healing, restoring, forgiving, and reconciling: it is not of God and His Kingdom… but of us. Our sinful ways are bent on breaking, dividing, fracturing, and harboring because it is only focused on one thing- what we want or what we can get.

I know people who profess Christ with their lips but who are careless with the words they use. Their words hurt, divide, embitter, tear-down, and wound other people and relationships. The ways of the kingdoms of the world teach us to argue back, make ourselves feel better by tearing others down, talk behind another's back, and curse someone who has wronged us. In the Kingdom of God, the Spirit gives us patience and self-control while gracing our words with encouragement, healing, and blessing for the building up of others.

God, how we need to repent of our selfishness, self-centeredness, and egocentrism that has been responsible for wounding, hurting, and forcing our ways and our agendas in our churches and our relationships rather than allowing the way of the Spirit to extend the rich, holistic, and healing way of the Kingdom of God. We have been set free and have been made new to live, to breathe, and to move forward in the freedom of the Spirit. Listen to me- we do not need more strategic visions, focus groups, or investigative teams to develop or research the feasibility or practicality of the way of Jesus and His Kingdom! We need men and women on their knees praying and asking for the Spirit to transform, lead, and shepherd us to be the embodiment of the Kingdom of God in every aspect of our lives for the sake of the world. Who will begin doing this? It must start with you!

Please don't misunderstand me in any of this. I am not pretending that I have not been a part of this problem in the past because I have. I will be the first to confess that I am a sinner in need for grace and forgiveness, but thanks to God I have seen the error in my way and in the error of our churches. I pray that we, together, may be on our knees repenting of our sinfulness and asking for the Spirit of God to move in us and through us in power.

In the Kingdom of God, there is a selfless Spirit that yearns to serve, build up, and love those in our relationships, in our fellowships, and in the larger world. In the Kingdom of God, it is an honor and a blessing to be in relationship and fellowship with other servant believers within our churches and communities. In the Kingdom of God, the Spirit guides our hearts and minds out of selfishness and teaches us the way of the selfless servant. In our homes, in our churches, and in the larger world, the follower of Christ should not look at what he or she is *receiving* as much as what he or she is *giving* to God and to his or her brothers and sisters in Christ, and to others. Let the Spirit guide the way we see others, so that we only see Christ in them, for it is to Christ to whom we give our love and service.

How We Lead

Whether you are someone who is a leader in your church or someone who does not know the first thing about Church leadership, it is important to know how our churches ought to be taken care of and shepherded. When the sheep are malnourished, sickly, and ravaged by predators it is the issue of the shepherds. Good shepherds have an intimate love for and knowledge of their flocks. They care for their sheep and tend to them in order to make sure they are healthy, strong, and protected. They guide them, watch over them, and care for them as their own.

In 2 Peter 2:25, the Christian is likened to a sheep that has gone astray but has returned to Christ, the Shepherd (*poimane*) and Overseer (*episkopos*) of our souls. Christ is the Good Shepherd who watches over those under His care. He feeds, cares for, and protects the sheep in His flock. Interestingly enough, Peter uses the same words- shepherd (*poimane*) and overseer (*episkopos*)- a few chapters later to describe those who have been entrusted the care of His flock within our churches. He was speaking directly to those who have taken on the task of watching over and caring for our churches. Peter writes to the elders in chapter 5, *"Be shepherds (poimane) of God's flock that is under your care, serving as overseers (episkopos)."*

The elders of our churches are to be Christ-like in the way they know their sheep, feed their sheep, care for their sheep, and protect their sheep from danger. They have been entrusted by Christ himself with the responsibility of His flock. And, they will be held accountable for the way they have or have not taken care of God's precious sheep. What an awesome and serious responsibility...and- one we have taken too lightly.

The elders within our churches have taken on new and different responsibilities than what God intended. In many ways they have come to resemble a corporate Board of Directors, directing the affairs of their employees and company. They manage the church staff and deal with legal issues, financial campaigns, building issues and projects, service times, new projects and services, and unhappy consumers. The elders have become the shepherds and overseers of the product that generates the income. As much as our leaders hate to admit it, they have to keep a stream of revenue coming in to cover the business operations and employees. Our elders work to minimize disruption in revenue and keep the church machine running. Sadly, this is the measure by which many of our churches have elected our eldership. Those who have selfless, relational and pastoral hearts, given over to the shepherding of the sheep, have not stepped forward. Or, when they have stepped forward, they have been molded, shaped, and influenced by the current mode of operation. What we end up with are "good people" who make "good" and "logical" business and financial decisions for our churches, but not shepherds who feed, care for, and protect the sheep.

This is a strong indictment, but one of which I am completely confident and resolute. I have seen this in small and large churches alike. Our elders, because of immense pressure to keep the church afloat and appease the consumers, have turned into something they were never intended to be, while doing things they were never intended to do. The elders within our churches are to be those who intimately shepherd and watch over the sheep in their flocks, in the way of Christ. They ought not to look at our churches as businesses. They do not run like a business. They do not need businessmen in order for it to work. The eldership is comprised of selfless servants who give their lives to prayer and the Spirit, nurturing and pouring themselves out for the care of their sheep. They are the caring and loving image of Christ within our churches who lead us in the ways of Christ.

It is essential that we stop to learn the lessons from Israel's past and how its shepherds wrongly cared for God's flock. By reading the strong indictments of the prophets in the Old Testament, one can find rather quickly that instead of tending to the needs of the God's flock by nurturing, caring, and protecting them, Israel's elders were all too concerned for their own interests and pursuits. It is for this reason that they came under the consternation and judgment of God.

> This is what the Sovereign LORD says: Woe to the shepherds of Israel who only take care of themselves! Should not shepherds take care of the flock? You eat the curds, clothe yourselves with the wool and slaughter the choice animals, but you do not take care of the flock. You have not strengthened the weak or healed the sick or bound up the injured. You have not brought back the strays or searched for the lost. You have ruled them harshly and brutally. So they were scattered because there was no shepherd, and when they were scattered they became food for all the wild animals. My sheep wandered over all the mountains and on every high hill. They were scattered over the whole earth, and no one searched or looked for them.

> Therefore, you shepherds, hear the word of the LORD: As surely as I live, declares the Sovereign LORD, because my flock lacks a shepherd and so has been plundered and has become food for all the wild animals, and because my shepherds did not search for my flock but cared for themselves rather than for my flock; therefore, O shepherds, hear the word of the LORD this is what the Sovereign LORD says: I am against the shepherds and will hold them accountable for my flock. I will remove them from tending the flock so that the shepherds can no longer feed themselves. Ezekiel 34: 2-10

The prophet Jeremiah continues:

> Woe to the shepherds who are destroying and scattering the sheep of my pasture!" declares the LORD. Therefore this is what the LORD, the God of Israel, says to the shepherds who tend my people: "Because you have scattered my flock and driven them away and have not bestowed care on them, I will bestow punishment on you for the evil you have done," declares the LORD. Jeremiah 23: 1-2

Elders, what words would God write to you in the way you have tended and cared for your flock? Would God bless your work or would He curse your work? Would Christ shepherd and watch over your church differently than you do? Would He be doing the same things as you, or would He do other things? Would His interests be the same as the interests you set for your church, or would they be different? Would His priorities for your church be the same as your priorities?

More specifically, do you know the people under your care by name? Do you know the intimate needs they have in their lives? Are you an active intercessor in their lives? Are you actively teaching and training them up in the way of Christ in all that they do? Are you nurturing and caring for them when they are sick or in need? Are you actively protecting them from the attacks of the enemy? Are you leading them into a Kingdom fellowship in which they embody righteousness and holiness in all they do, helping them grow daily in the way of the Good Shepherd? Are you on your knees leading your Church in humble, contrite, and submissive prayer? Are you leading those around you in a top-down approach, or are you coming up from the bottom to nurture and serve?

Or, have you been more interested in the growth and status of your church? Are you more concerned with the status of *your* position within the church? Are you more concerned with daily operations of your church than the spiritual development of the people under your care? Are you more concerned with the next building expansion plan and the way your church will finance it or with the spiritual foundation of those in your midst? Have you given more of your time to business meetings in which you discuss staff issues and member complaints than meeting in the homes of those in your care? Do you spend more time mulling over the next big thing or considering the next program rather than nurturing and building up your congregation to spiritual health? Do you spend more time putting out fires and letting misguided people in your church beat you and other pastors in your church around because they are not getting what they want, or do you speak the truth in love to them for their individual spiritual health and the spiritual health of your church?

If the Church is to be the embodiment of new creation, a sign post of God's rule and God's reign in our lives here and now, who will nurture and guide us along the way? Who will gather together the lost and sickly sheep and bring them back into the fold to be whole and healed? Who will lead us into the way of Christ and guide us into rich Kingdom lives? Our churches desperately need to rethink the role and responsibility of those who lead us. We need a fresh beginning by throwing out the ways and practices of sinful man that God despises. We instead need to pray for true, authentic shepherds within our fellowships who are wholly dependant on the power of God in all matters.

We need shepherds in our churches who actively pray for and seek the moving of the Holy Spirit when we gather together. We need shepherds who are not afraid to practice and live out their faith for fear that it might seem too weird or that it might frighten off the people we are "trying to get to join our churches." We need shepherds who operate in the power of the Holy Spirit rather than operate in the power, convention, and "wisdom" of men. We need shepherds who guide us fearlessly in the power of the Spirit, rather than those who lead and make decisions based upon what they think is right or what they want. We need shepherds who recognize that the Body of Christ does not need additional heads, for Christ's headship is sufficient. We need shepherds who will be completely submissive to the headship of Christ.

We need shepherds who move and operate at an organic level in the midst of their flock rather than elders who have turned their churches into corporations that need corporate leadership. We need shepherds who guide, teach, and train up a movement of servants (*diakonis*) to serve within our churches. We need shepherds who will preach, teach, and call their churches to the way of Christ and His Kingdom rather than accommodate and coddle those who just want to *play* church. We need shepherds who understand that the Kingdom of God is not a matter of words but a matter of power, and that power only comes from our Heavenly Father through His Holy Spirit given freely to those who are asking, seeking, and knocking.

Good shepherds do not stand in front of the flock blocking them or beating them into submission. Good shepherds guide their sheep to embody the Kingdom of God and move in freedom, guiding them out into the world in order to spread wildly the Good News of this Kingdom, never holding them back by rules, regulations, protocols, traditions, bureaucracies, fear, or intimidation. God give us courage to change the ways we lead. Forgive us for how we have abused our positions of leadership and give us good shepherds who will shepherd us like Christ.

You

As Holy Spirit begins to change our hearts, we see everything differently. We begin to see people and situations differently. We no longer divide people into classes and categories. We see people for who they are, beautifully and wonderfully created sons and daughters of God. This is how we begin to see our friends and enemies. This is also how we begin to put ourselves among, not just the rich or middle-class, but the poor as well. Our hearts become compassionate toward both the miserable rich man and the beggar on the street corner without judging either for his situation. We care for and join those whom the world views as the scum of the earth because we have become the servant of all.[66]

The Spirit gives us the very heart of Christ and we begin to love the outcasts of the world, even if it is not popular in the world or within our churches. The love of God captures our hearts and we extend love, mercy, and compassion for people no matter the sin-group. We see people clearly for who they are and who we are: as children of God who have fallen short of His glory. We do not judge them for we recognize that our own sin is no better than theirs. We walk beside them in grace and love, revealing Christ to them each step of the way so that they too may follow.

This kind of grace and love means that our thoughts, actions, and attitudes have to change toward those who are not like us. We ought to be individuals and churches who are in the midst of, and always welcoming, those who do not know Christ at all. We ought to find those who curse, get drunk, get high, tell inappropriate jokes, sleep around, and live completely untransformed lives coming into our fellowships because they are looking for something greater than what they have settled for in their lives. And not one of them ought to be judged, scoffed at, or turned away. We have not been called to be their judges. Rather, we have been called to demonstrate the way of the Kingdom through humble, graceful, self-sacrificial love to every person of the world. We, as broken sinners, walk beside other broken sinners of the world and invite them into a new and better way of life that is experienced in the Kingdom of God.

We also learn to let go of our need to defend, control, and hold on to power over other people. Instead, we begin to learn the Christ-like way of becoming submissive, gentle, loving, peaceful, and graceful. Our disposition begins to change when we submit to God's way. We, again, recognize that the place God would have us is at the bottom, below everyone else in the world, so as to come up from below everyone in humility and service. In the Kingdom of God, the last will be first and the first will be last. We should not assume the position of honor at the front table rather we take the unassuming table in the back of the room. This is the way of Jesus Christ and His Kingdom.

There cannot be enough emphasis on this truth for Kingdom people: *we must become people of the bottom; people who are below; people who are last; people who are in the back; people who are the least.* We are people who put the interest of others before ourselves becoming a servant to all- our friends, our spouses, our children, our brothers and sisters in Christ, those wildly different than us, and our enemies- in order to demonstrate the love of God. We are not loud, showy, boisterous, obnoxious, or holier-than-thou. We simply follow the low and humble way of the suffering servant and we do it in every situation or context, for the low and humble way changes hearts and minds.

As such, we are transformed to be like Christ to the unfair boss, the slow store clerk, the rude or obnoxious salesperson, the junkie on the street, and the antagonistic loudmouth. We are loving, patient, and long-suffering to those who offend, trespass, or violate us. God's love bursts forth from our lives in such a remarkable and profound way that the world is drawn to this Christ whom they have never known before because they see Him demonstrated through us. In our own power we do not have the capacity to act in such profound ways; it is only by the power of God working through us that we are able. It is never us, only God.

Too many times I believe that we as Christians become so identified with the culture of our churches and "the way we have always done things" that we leave the way of Jesus in the dust without ever thinking much about it. We have enabled, rather than confronted, the small, petty antics that hardly look like Jesus and His Kingdom. Think about how misaligned and feeble our ways are and how petty our ways look compared to the awesome, transformative, and magnetic ways of Christ and His Kingdom.

We say we are Christians, but we judge people who walk into our church services by who they are, how they are dressed, how they look, or how much money they have. The ways of the kingdoms of the world divides people into classes and judges them for who they are, what they have done, and what they have or don't have. In the Kingdom of God there is no judgment because we only see others as the children of God. We also recognize that we are the "chief of all sinners" not any better or any worse than anyone else.[67]

We say we are Christians, but we are easily hurt or offended by our brothers and sisters in our churches. Rather than walking the pathway of humility, peace, and reconciliation we run away to other churches and hide from our issues. The ways of the kingdoms of the world encourage pouting and resentment when one gets his feelings hurt. In the Kingdom of God we work toward humility, submission, and forgiveness with anyone and everyone who speaks poorly of us, hurts us, offends us, or even strikes us.

We say we are Christians, but when we are not officially recognized by the preacher for our service, or accomplishment, we get our feelings hurt. The ways of the kingdoms of the world promote accomplishment, recognition, and accolades for a job well done. In the Kingdom of God we are happy and joyful when we can serve our God in secret; in such a way that the right hand does not know what the left hand is doing.

We say we are Christians, but when we are not in agreement with a church decision we withhold our offering in protest or organize to force our own way and agenda. The ways of the kingdoms of the world are bent on political power and influence and teach us that it is best to manipulate in order to get what we want. In the Kingdom of God we pray together in unity for the Spirit of God to be our guide, so that we may bear with each other in grace and love. We carry each other's burdens while seeking God on our knees in prayer together.

We say we are Christians, but many times we are negative about someone else or something within the church and work to divide one person against another. The ways of the kingdoms of the world work to fracture, hurt, and divide individuals and relationships, pitting one person or group against each other. In the Kingdom of God we work toward the uplifting, encouragement, and building up of each person in his or her life and relationships. We work toward the healing and the restoration of people, relationships, and church bodies.

We say we are Christians, but we are always demanding the way we like things, forcing our own individual way and our own individual agenda on others and the church. The ways of the kingdoms of the world teach us to look out for our own interests, the survival of the fittest, and the necessity of taking care of "numero uno." In the Kingdom of God we work together in unity considering the interests of others before our own while making sure that each person is taken care of and ministered to...*most especially* the weakest and most modest parts of the Body among us.[68]

It is the "minister" who seeks attention and puts his way before others in order to receive special recognition from the congregation. The ways of the kingdoms of the world promote and give special attention to great leaders for their accomplishments and accolades, celebrating the achievements of one man. In the Kingdom of God each part of the Body is equally important with no one part being any more important than another. Each part of the body uses his or her God-given gifts, with all praise and attention going to God. As a result, each of us ought to submit to one another, washing one another's feet in humility and service as Christ would do for us.

The list of examples could go on and on forever, but don't miss the point. As followers of Christ, as those who have been made new by the Holy Spirit, as those who operate by a new set of standards in the Kingdom of God, we must confront and die to the wicked ways of the world and be the Church God has made us to be. For His salvation has allowed us to embody not the old, worn-out, and self-interested ways of the kingdoms of the world, but the Life-giving Kingdom of God. And we live this way every second of the day.

Praise God that He can move in such spectacular ways in spite of our lack of cooperation. Praise God that He does not give up on us when we continue to fall so miserably short of His ways. Praise God that, even now, He continues to patiently wait for each of us to surrender our hearts and our lives to His reign and His rule and His Kingdom!

Inside Out

The words on these pages are not enough to transform you. Inspirational and motivational words are energizing, but they are not enough to sustain your fleeting emotions and not powerful enough to completely change you at the core of your being. Sure they may lift you up and get you excited for a bit, but those feelings will soon fade and you will remain untransformed in your life.

It is only in a life centered on Jesus Christ and the moment by moment sacrifice of your will and your way to the Spirit of God that you begin to change inwardly. When this happens, the Kingdom begins to break out through your life in power. It is only through your continual and perpetual worship that the Kingdom begins to reign inwardly then outwardly in your life. The Kingdom seed is planted. It takes root. It grows wildly. It bears fruit.

We must understand from the beginning that it is not about what you can do in your own power, but rather what the power of God can do to transform you. It is not about what you can do outwardly to be a better Christian; rather it is coming face to face with Jesus Christ and His in-breaking Kingdom that begins to change you inwardly. It is allowing Christ to come so close that your heart, your mind, your desires, and your feelings begin to change. It is the easiest (and hardest thing) you will ever do, but it is essential to understand that you do not have the capacity to live a righteous and holy life in your own power, rather it is only when you are reborn from the inside that God's ways become your own.

You must pray for the Spirit to come into your heart and your life, for that is the only place where transformation can begin and the only place where the Kingdom can take root and reign. It is a spiritual problem that needs a spiritual solution and it can only be cured by the Spirit of God. When the Spirit comes close and begin to works intimately in your life, you begin changing. You are able to see the world as God sees the world. You hunger for those things which God hungers. You pursue those things which God pursues. You desire those things which God desires. You cannot get enough of Jesus and His way and His Kingdom. You change so radically from the inside that the power of the Spirit cannot help but work its way out into your life in *everything* you do. But sacrifice and surrender to God the Holy Spirit is essential.

The way of Jesus always means sacrifice. It is a sacrifice in which you become so hidden in the fullness of Christ that it is no longer you, only Him. It is never what *you* can do; it is only what can be done *through* you when you get out of the way. It is essential for each of us to pray and plead to God for a transformation from the inside and for a deep hunger for His Kingdom to come into our lives and work through each of us.

Just five years ago I did not know much about the Bible. I did not have any passion or excitement to read it. My guess is that I was a lot like many Christians today; the thought of reading my Bible seemed more like a chore than anything life-giving. One day I began to pray that God would change my heart and that I would have a passion and a hunger for Him and His Word. In ways that I can only explain as miraculous, my heart and my life began to change. I began to have a hunger for anything and everything of God.

I wanted to pray without ceasing. I wanted to give up my own pursuits and desires. I wanted to read and understand more about God. I wanted to know what God was doing in and through my life for others. The changes in my life didn't come from guilting myself to death. It didn't come from arm-twisting or beating myself into submission. My inner passion, desire, and hunger came from God emptying me of me and filling me with His Spirit. That is when I began to find Life and began to understand the words of Jesus, "I came that [you] might have Life and have it abundantly." I wholly believe that for any one of us to change, it has to begin in humility, selflessness, repentance, and sacrifice of our own ways coupled with an insatiable hunger and desire for God to come close and change our hearts and minds. It is then that the Spirit is invited to begin the transformative work of raising you to new Life.

But how deeply inside our lives do we allow the Spirit to work? How much of ourselves do we really fully sacrifice? Are there certain places within you that are off limits? Are there certain areas that have been purposefully blocked off? Are there areas of darkness that you keep hidden because it is just too difficult or too embarrassing to go there? You have to admit, we rarely ask questions like these in our churches. It is as if we are all completely cool with a superficial scrub of the house, but we are reluctant to open up all of the windows and doors to the house and even more reluctant to open the closets inside. The truth is that the entire house needs cleaning, but we have to be willing to open all the windows and doors and every single closet for the work to begin.

For me, words like humility, selflessness, repentance, and sacrifice had always been these abstract words that really didn't mean anything for my life. I knew that a Christian ought to exhibit those qualities, but it was just a mental thing, not a real way of living. In essence, I was comfortable opening a couple of windows and doors for the Spirit to come into, but I kept the shades drawn and other doors securely locked deep inside. Not only was there no possibility of cleaning the restricted areas, I would not even allow the Light to break in.

One evening I brought together a handful of my Christian brothers from my church. I told them how important it is that we come together as sinners at the foot of the cross to confess our sins to God and to each other in repentance. The truth is that it was my way of finally opening up every window, door, and closet that had remained closed and off limits.

It was my way of finally exposing every bit of darkness within me to the Light of Christ.

In the presence of God and my Christian brothers, I began to verbally confess every sin I could remember in my life. All of the windows were opening and every door to the house invited in my dear Friend. Humility, selflessness, repentance, and sacrifice became a real part of my life as I began carrying the cross of Christ. I went through every room, kicked down every closet door, and asked my Friend to do the work I was completely incapable of doing. The pockets of darkness that had been hidden deep in my life and that kept the Light of Christ from penetrating my heart had now been opened up. The cleaning of the entire house could now begin. There was no longer a place for the darkness to hide. The Light of Christ broke into my heart and began to transform me into a new man.

The man who had been the cheater, the liar, the adulterer, the perverse, the foul-mouthed, the self-centered, and the verbal abuser had been exposed, put to death, and forgiven by Christ and my brothers. It was evident that there was absolutely nothing spectacular about me, only Christ in me. I had never felt so much appreciation and gratitude for Christ and His love for me. I also had never felt so much appreciation and gratitude for the Spirit that began to do the work in my life that I could never do and to teach me new and higher ways. Life completely changed for me that night.

Are you willing to open not just the windows and doors, but also the closets that you have kept hidden deep within your life? Are you willing to let the Light break into those hidden places so that the Light of Christ will begin to shine through you? Are you willing to let the "old man" be exposed so that the new man might come to life? Are you willing to lead by example the way of humility, selflessness, repentance, and sacrifice by being confessional with your other brothers and sisters in Christ so that they may see you not as someone who is perfect, but as a sinner who is forgiven and who is being made new? For the Spirit to begin the deepest cleaning, you must be willing to walk the sacrificial pathway of Christ for transformation to begin. It is only on this pathway where Christ and His Kingdom together are glorified in and through your entire life.

The Kingdom in Community

The Spirit is magnetic in how Kingdom people are drawn together. The very foundation of our faith rests in the communal, triune God breaking in to the lives of broken vessels in order to restore wholeness and unity in our relationships, first with Him and then each other. We become individuals who gravitate toward each other in community. We live life with each other daily. We share and celebrate with one another by praying and worshiping when we gather together. We encourage and build up one another in Christ every opportunity we have. We walk gracefully with one another when we are sinned against, always extending forgiveness and working toward reconciliation in our relationships with one another. This kind of community cannot be something we casually participate in when we gather together on Sundays, as if we are dipping our toe into the water to see how it feels. The very heart of the Kingdom of God is life with one another, and there is no greater privilege or opportunity on earth.

Many years ago I was responsible for teaching people within a church the heart of Christian community lived outside of Sunday services. I was given the task of organizing and encouraging small group gatherings throughout the week. While I was encouraged that there was positive movement by many to begin meeting with one another throughout the week, I was surprised by a few things. First, I was surprised that such a large percentage within the church did not want to be in community together outside of the Sunday service. Second, I was surprised how many people told me that they didn't have time to meet with their Christian brothers and sisters throughout the week. And third, I was surprised that many of the groups that did begin meeting only wanted to meet bi-weekly or monthly with each other. It was certainly a step in the right direction to begin meeting, but it was still far from the heart of begin a vibrant Christian community that is in each other's presence regularly.

There is nothing inherently wrong with us gathering together weekly for our Sunday services in a centralized location, but more importantly and more essentially, our gatherings must also be spread and scattered into our homes and our neighborhoods. The heart and lifeblood of the Christian community of believers cannot be wholly dependent upon centralized gatherings at our church building. In fact, moving away from our church building is the future of the Church, and it must begin to be our present reality. Meeting with our brothers and sisters in Christ throughout the week ought not to be viewed as inferior or second-order to our weekly gatherings. Meeting and gathering with one another throughout the week in our homes is even more important than Sunday church service. It is in the smaller, relational settings where we don't just *learn* how to be the Church, it is where we actually begin *living* as the Church. It is the place where we can still worship, pray, learn, give testimony, and break bread with each other, but also the place where we begin to live and demonstrate they way of Christ in grace, forgiveness, reconciliation, and self-sacrificial love.

The reason life outside the centralized church building is the best place to demonstrate and live out the way of Christ is that we very quickly find out that there is no such thing as perfect people or perfect Christian community. We recognize that we are all sinners saved by the grace of God and that each one of us is at a different place in our spiritual walk, which can only mean one thing- that my Christian brother or sister will sin against me at some point. And while it is hard to even contemplate, *I* may even sin against someone at some point as well! The ability and commitment to work through our sins and failures is evidence that we have been united as one through the Father and Son and have made a commitment to one another to walk the way of Christ despite our shortcomings. What a glorious demonstration of Kingdom community and the embodiment of new creation!

Our church mode of operation has been quite different than the way of the Kingdom. The way we respond to someone who fails us, sins against us, or violates us within our churches is avoidance, jumping ship, or running to a different church. Taking the hard road of Christ in demonstrating and extending peace, forgiveness, and reconciliation has not been our norm. The truth is that we have not done a very good job of teaching people that Kingdom community is not only lived out and experienced through the highs of life, but also through the very lows of life. It is in both places where we begin to learn and embody the way of Christ and His Kingdom. It is completely unrealistic to believe that things will always be perfect in our church communities, no matter how hyped up or exciting they may be. People will hurt us and fail us because we are all learning how to die to ourselves and how to depend on the power of the Holy Spirit to make us like Christ in all things, even in community with one another.

I am in community with people who are *learning* to walk the way of Christ in the power of the Spirit every moment. These same people are a bunch of imperfect sinners who are all full of misgivings. I see them stumble in the same sins each day while hurting each other with their words and action, many times only looking out for their own self-interest. As a result, I have learned, and am continuing to learn, new depths of grace and mercy as I walk beside them on the pathway of Christ. Not surprisingly, they too are learning new depths of grace and mercy toward me, as I am not exempt from these same mistakes myself. What a blessing to be in graceful, merciful, and loving fellowship with brothers and sisters who do not just want to worship Christ, but take on His yoke in their lives.

To be honest it would just be easier to give up on each other, as if some of us are more righteous or less sinful than our brothers and sisters. But since God has extended His abounding grace, mercy, and love to each of us as unworthy sinners, who are we to not do the same for a brother or sister who has wronged or sinned against us? As citizens of the Kingdom of God, do we run away from and give up on our brothers and sisters with whom we have conflict, or do we take the lonely road of forgiveness and reconciliation?

Within the last year our church eldership found out about some marital infidelity between a married man and a married woman in our church. As a result, one of the couples left our community while the other couple stayed. The entire situation was, and continues to be, a massive punch to the gut. It is hard enough to see the people you love suffering in their marriages, but to also see them suffering in the relationship they used to have with each other and within our church community is unbearable.

It is like taking the most expensive and exquisite glass vase to the top of a spiral staircase and then dropping it onto the marble floor below. Not only is it difficult to see something so beautiful and valuable shattered to pieces, it is difficult to find all of the broken and fractured pieces and even more difficult still to begin putting them back together.

The broken pieces of infidelity were scattered everywhere. Some of the larger and more obvious pieces were easy to identify. We began meeting with each family individually in order to get them into marital counseling. As you can imagine, working through betrayal and trust issues can very easily break up a marriage. By the grace of God, each couple was committed to the long and messy process of cleaning up the shattered pieces and the difficult task of putting them back together.

In their marriages, they committed to walk the road of the Kingdom by extending grace, mercy, and forgiveness to their sinful spouses. Through tears and hard, truthful conversations with each other, the Spirit began the process of healing their marriages. While the wisdom of the kingdoms of the world say to retaliate, divorce, and hold grudges, the Kingdom of God works toward forgiveness, reconciliation, and healing.

But the road to forgiveness, reconciliation, and healing simply could not end with the marriages alone. The ripple effect of the sin started with each individual and marriage but moved outward further fracturing friendships and relationships.

By avoiding forgiveness and reconciliation in the other relationships, it would be equivalent to taking the four largest broken pieces and gluing them back together without including any of the smaller pieces. It would begin to resemble the beautiful vase, but it would leave too many gaps and cracks. The vase would be significantly incomplete.

Even though no one within our church at the time knew about the infidelity (because we wanted it to come straight from the mouths of each person involved), each individual and couple was spiritually suffering by feeling cut off and disconnected from Christian community. It wasn't that anyone was treating them differently; no one knew about it. But the weight of guilt and shame they carried made them feel alone. They desperately needed to be connected to God and to their Christian family.

Sweeping these kinds of issues under the rug or hoping that they will go away is not the best we can do in our churches. Sin is bent on isolating, dividing, and destroying relationships and the individual. Sin separates us from Christ and from each other. Sin breaks up Christian community and pits each one of us against the other. So whether it is infidelity in a relationship or just conflict between friends, the answer is not ignoring it, but working through it together.

It is only when we confess our sins to one another and to God that sin loses its power, the barriers are removed, and we are welcomed back into union with Christ and our brothers and sisters in Christ. This is the pathway that the follower of Christ must walk in Christian community, and this is precisely what we did.

Although it may was one of the most heart-wrenching experiences I have ever been through, each person came before the church and confessed his and her sin. Each one read a letter that detailed the sin and that asked for forgiveness from God and from the church. Tears accompanied their heartbroken words as they poured their repentant hearts out. There wasn't a dry eye in the room, as we all could hear ourselves reading those words. We too were the sinners, and we could do nothing less than forgive them of their sin and pray for them and their families.

Since then, our elders have continued to meet with each person involved in order to continue putting the pieces back together. This is not something will happen in the snap of a finger or a click of the heels. Submitting our wills and our ways and trusting God to work through the broken pieces is a long and arduous process, but it is precisely how the Church lives in community with one another and embodies the Kingdom of God. We commit to following the way of Christ in community in both the easy times and the hard times.

But, who are the people who surround you in order to speak truth into your life on a daily basis? Who are the people you trust to ask you the tough questions in order to keep you above reproach? Whom are you actively seeking and inviting to hold you accountable to the way of Christ and His Kingdom? These questions are essential.

God uses each of us in Christian community to speak the truth in love to each other. This is one of the ways that God works and moves to refine us into Christ. I am a sinner and far from perfect. I need those who are in community with me telling me when they see the "old man" creeping up and showing his ugly face. You see, I ought to hate the "old man" so much that I seek out my brothers and sisters to tell me when they see him creeping back to life in my thoughts, actions, or attitudes.

In Christian community, we must all remove the prideful chips that we put on our shoulders. When my Christian brothers or sisters tell me that they see the "old man" in me, it is because they love me and are trying to help me. It isn't because they are trying to hurt, wound, or offend me. We miss their intentions too many times because of our pride and arrogance.

God, our communities are in desperate need of selfless souls who love each other and seek out the Truth in love and who can hear Truth in love without egos and attitudes. Please forgive us for our arrogance, pride, and love of our sin and waywardness. Give us hearts that welcome the truth told to us in love.

I remember one Monday last year when I received an email from a young lady I really respect in our church. She apologized that she had not taken the opportunity before to tell me how much she appreciated the gifts I bring to our community. She went further with her apology by saying that this particular email was not for the sake of telling me how much she appreciates me, but for the sake of confronting me with careless words that I chose to use one Sunday.

How ought we respond to such things as Kingdom people? Do we get wildly offended that a person would have the nerve to say such things? Do we get ticked that the person only wants to write us when we do something wrong and not when we do something good or right? Do we respond in anger, resentment, and hostility toward this person and then try to avoid her in the future? Do we justify our words, actions, and behavior and then think of the things we could say to retaliate? The answer to all of these questions is an obvious NO.

In the Kingdom of God we recognize our sinfulness and the way we fail not only God, but our brothers and sisters in Christ. We recognize that we are no better than the other sinners in our midst and we join each of them under the foot of the cross, confessing our sins, and asking for God's forgiveness and for the forgiveness of those we have sinned against. The way of the Kingdom is recognizing our lowly position below everyone else and then welcoming the loving rebuke of our brothers and sisters.

In this instance, even though the "old man" wanted to creep back to life, I humbled myself, prayed for the Spirit to teach me the ways of Christ, and then took the low and humble road of Christ and His Kingdom in my response. I called the young lady and told her how much I appreciated her care for me as a brother in Christ. I confessed to her (and then later to the church) my sinfulness, and asked for forgiveness from God, her, and my church family. Praise God that there are Christian brothers and sisters in my community who love me enough to extend grace, mercy, forgiveness, and the very love of God when I fall short without giving up on me. The more fully hidden in Christ we are, the easier it is for Him to extend His grace, mercy, forgiveness, and love through us in Christian community.

Life in Christian community is far, far from perfect, but it is the place where we display the Kingdom of God for the world to see. It is the place where we make a commitment to stand beside one another, even when it is tough. It is the place where we learn how to be a Christ-centered community, especially *when we fail each other*. And, it is the place where we give praise to God for the way He is working in spite of us. Dietrich Bonhoeffer writes in his classic work on Christian community, *Life Together:*

> We pray for the big things and forget to give thanks for the small (and yet really not small) gifts. How can God entrust great things to one who will not thankfully receive from Him the little things? If we do not give thanks daily for the Christian fellowship in which we have been placed, even where there is no great experience, no discoverable riches, but much weakness, small faith, and difficulty; if on the contrary, we only keep complaining to God that everything is so paltry and petty, so far from what we expected, then we hinder God from letting our fellowship grow according to the measure and riches which are there for all of us in Jesus Christ.[69]

Outward and Onward

The Kingdom of God must be lived and demonstrated outside of the four walls of the church building. The Kingdom of God must extend into our neighborhoods, town centers, restaurants, coffee shops, bars and pubs, hospitals, jailhouses, nursing homes, and into every place outside of our centralized location. The Kingdom of God must extend in the midst of our friends, neighbors, co-workers, new acquaintances, and our enemies alike. The mindset of "taking my friend to church so the minister can preach to him" is old school thinking. It is not wrong; it is just not the best we can do.

We are a royal priesthood, a holy nation that is commissioned to go into the entire world, teaching, demonstrating, and giving testimony to how God is making all things new.[70] We are the living, breathing testimony of what God can do to save, and we must take that message everywhere we go. We *must* be in the midst of the world to demonstrate it. We must open up our welcoming homes and get to know those in our neighborhoods and towns. We must take the Kingdom of God to the people, for they have stopped coming to us in our church buildings.

I have dear friends who left the United States a year ago in order to be missionaries in Torino, Italy. They have spent their time over the last year meeting and developing real relationships with people in their neighborhood, including local business owners, by frequenting coffee shops and cafés near their apartment. Since they do not have a minister or church building in which to bring people, they have had to be among them, becoming a living testimony of God's love and Kingdom in the way they talk, live, and relate to everyone. They take the Kingdom *to* people by living it and breathing it through their lives.

One day, my friends were with a large group of Italians who began to ask why they were in Italy. My friend told them that they came to Italy in order to share their faith and salvation in Jesus Christ. Someone in the group then asked, "So where is your church?" Before my friend could even begin to answer the question, Mario, a local business owner with whom my friends had developed a relationship over the last year, responded to the man, "Do you see these streets? This is his church. Do you see these restaurants? This is his church. Do you see these people? This is his church."

Mario absolutely nailed it, and what a fantastic testimony to the work my friends are doing to teach the Italian people about what the Church ought to be. We in the Church must begin to see the Church like Mario sees the Church. We must begin to see the Church differently than we have in the past. We must begin to move away from our church buildings that have propped us and have kept us from the great missional task of the Church in the neighborhoods and streets of the world.

It is no longer acceptable to weigh down our churches with significant overhead costs in salaries, benefits, mortgages, and so on. This may freak some of you out, but it is essential that we begin to rethink how we are organized, how our resources are used, and how this compares to our lives in the Kingdom of God. We must reduce our dependence on money to keep our churches afloat and begin to teach and train the people under our care the importance of being the Church away from a centralized building, while also reducing their dependence on a church staff.

The consumerist Christian mentality we have created, the Christian spectator sport, does not align with the Kingdom of God being embodied, lived out, and taken to the world in word and deed. Again, it starts with each one of us. Instead of always facing inward, we must begin to face outward and onward to extend the Kingdom of God. In doing so, we will find that the things we once viewed as important on Sunday mornings are really not that important in comparison to the great spiritual needs of our time.

I am not advocating that large weekly, centralized gatherings are bad; they are not. But I am strongly advocating that we learn how to confront consumerist Christianity and that we learn how to be the Church away from our buildings while reducing our dependence upon them. I am strongly advocating that we teach and train those under our care, empowering them so as to not be dependent upon one single leader or staff team in order to be the Church. We must encourage and empower those under our care to live Kingdom lives in the power of the Spirit while releasing them to live the self-giving Gospel outside of the confines of our buildings.

This is why it is so important to have elders who are preoccupied with shepherding the flock. The flock is moving; it is mobile. A shepherd knows where the sheep are and then feeds, cares for, and protects them as they are grazing in the homes and neighborhoods of our towns and cities. Please hear me on this: *there is nothing more important at this time than for our leaders to begin teaching the importance of decentralizing our churches, meeting in our homes in celebration of Jesus in Word and Sacrament, and taking the Kingdom of God out into the world everywhere we go and in everything we do.* The centralized, top-heavy organization of our churches is not sustainable for the future- and not the best we can do for the Kingdom of God.

It is imperative for those under our care to learn the importance of using his or her gifts, talents, and abilities for the building up of others, not just in our churches but in our communities. We must encourage each person to understand that he or she is an integral part of the Body of Christ and must use his or her giftedness for the strengthening and extending of the Kingdom of God. The Kingdom of God is not about the vision, leadership, or strategy of one person or one small group of people. The Kingdom of God is a collection of people using their gifts, whether it is teaching, singing, encouragement, shepherding, or any number of gifts, in order to be a living, breathing in-breaking representation of heaven on earth. We use our God-given gifts to bless and build up those in our midst.

We must take those gifts and talents that God has so richly given us into the world to demonstrate the love and care of Jesus Christ. If you are a prayer warrior, don't just pray with your church family but walk the streets and pray for people and families you come in contact with. If you bless those within your church with encouragement and hospitality by writing letters and baking pies, then also write letters and bake pies for those in your neighborhood who could use some encouragement and conversation.

If you are a great listener and have a heart for those within your church who have experienced great pain and hurt, then volunteer at an organization in your town where you can provide solace and share the love of Christ to those who have been abandoned or victimized. If you love to share about Jesus Christ with those in your church, then share Christ to those outside of your church who are in prison, homeless shelters, and hospitals. If you are a great singer and love to sing praises to Jesus Christ in your church, then take your voice of praise to children's homes, nursing homes, a widow's home, or even out to the street corners! Let the Spirit work through your life to use the gifts God has given you to demonstrate His love and extend His light into every dark place on earth.

Your Kingdom Come

There has never been a more important time in history for the Church to learn the way of the Kingdom of God than right now. We are standing on a great precipice in history, anticipating something that is bigger than we could ever imagine for the sake of the world. *It is the unearthing of the treasure of the Kingdom of God embodied in the Church and touching the entire world.*

The very Kingdom that Christ preached and embodied is now coming to life in a repentant and resurrected Church. It is this united Church who will be transformed in thought, action, and deed, and who will come together and transcend cheap religion, petty bickering, and in-fighting, so that the entire world will once and for all know about the love, grace, and mercies of God, the Supremacy and Lordship of Jesus Christ, and the Life and Freedom in His Kingdom demonstrated through His people. We are breaking down the gates of hell and every stronghold that stands in our way! We have been empowered by God to go into all parts of the house and reclaim what is rightfully His. We move forward in the self-sacrificial way of Jesus Christ as we demonstrate the love, justice, mercy, and righteousness of our Lord and Savior.

Can the Kingdom of God transform the Church and change the world? It can, but it begins with you. You have the opportunity to turn from your sin, jump in the waters of baptism, and be completely transformed by the Holy Spirit of God. You have the opportunity to join this Kingdom movement that is turning the ways and workings of the world completely upside-down. You have the opportunity of a lifetime to give your heart, mind, body, and soul to the greatest movement that the world has ever seen. You have the opportunity to be a part of the greatest victory and story that will ever be told. But, the key to unlocking the glorious riches of the Kingdom of God lies with you!

Please, do not hold on to this book. Keep passing it to others so that they too will discover the riches of the Kingdom of God!

A Deeper Look

Jesus
How would re-centering Jesus in your life:
Change your individual priorities in life?
Change your perceived wants and needs in life?

How would re-centering Jesus in your church:
Change your church's priorities?
Change your church's wants and perceived needs?
Change style and preference and lead to unity your church?
Transform your church gatherings each time you meet together?

Holy Spirit
How would sacrificing your will and way, instead depending on the Spirit, begin to:
Change your life?
Change your relationships with other people?
Change your heart and how you see people?
Change your expectations of your church and church family?

How would your church be transformed and how would it look if:
It was full of the Holy Spirit?
It was led by the Holy Spirit?
Your church gatherings were led by the Holy Spirit?

Church Leadership
How does the Kingdom of God:
Change your church?
Change how your church spends money and resources?
Change how your church spends its time?
Change what your church prioritizes?
Change your approach to church leadership?
Change how your church will be led?
Change how you encourage? motivate? inspire? your church to action?

Change what you are preaching and teaching about?
Change the demographic to which your church is reaching out?
Change how your church cooperates and works with other churches?
Change the mission that your church has in the community and in the world?

You
How would re-centering Jesus and His Kingdom in your life:
Change your individual priorities in life?
Change your perceived wants and needs in life?
Change the way you speak to people?
Change what you talk about?
Change your thoughts about situations and people?
Change what you value in life?
Change your finances?
Change your priorities?
Change how you spend your time?
Change how you look at creation?

Dating, Marriage, and Family
How does the Kingdom:
Change your dating habits and/or behaviors?
Change your marriage?
Change how you raise your children?
Change your family time?
Change your purpose as a family?

Relationships
How does the Kingdom:
Change your temperament with others?
Change the grace you give others?
Change your judgment of others?
Change the grudges you hold toward others?
Change your forgiveness of others?
Change your need to retaliate (physically/verbally)?
Change your service to others?

The World
How does the Kingdom:
Change your hope, faith, and trust in politics?

Change your allegiance to any one country, president, or leader?

Change your your views of capitalism, socialism, communism, and other ideologies?

Change those things that you choose to defend and protect?

Change your views on social issues like homelessness, poverty, drug addiction, etc.?

Change your views on issues such as the death penalty, war, abortion, immigration, and weapons?

Change your views on global hunger, disease, and the poor?

Change your views on our stewardship of the earth?

Share Your Stories

As God begins to help you answer these questions, please visit www.theunearthedproject.com to share your stories of how the power of the Kingdom of God is transforming you, your family, your friends, your church, your community, and the world. Let us work together throughout the world, lifting each other up in prayer and encouragement, sharing stories and singing praises of the great God who is working through His body to rebuild the great wall that has been torn down for so long.

A Prayer of Reconciliation to the World

Father God,

Too many times we as Christians have been the loudest and most vocal voices and many times we have not represented or embodied the way, life, and teachings of your Son Jesus. Our judgmental and condemning voices have become a poor representation of Jesus in the community and the larger world and have left many who do not know anything about Jesus with a bad taste in their mouths and a deep contempt for your Church.

Too many times we are quick to say that we are the "defenders of the faith," or the "protectors of our Christians heritage." Yet in our zealousness to defend, we have compromised the way of your son, Jesus, and have many times done it in his name.

Father we repent and ask for forgiveness, for we know that Jesus did not spend his time isolating and targeting special "sin groups" or trying to defend his positions through arguing and debating.

Father we ask humbly that you replace our ways with your ways. For we know that the way of Jesus does not have to be defended; it must be demonstrated. It never moves out in judgment; it moves out in love. It never extends in condemnation to the world; it extends in grace and mercy. The ways of arguing, defending, judging, and condemning always build up walls and embitters those in the world who are on the receiving end. For every way that we as the Church have fallen short of representing you to the world, we ask for forgiveness.

Father, we are so eager to accept your grace, but are so unwilling to extend it. We are so eager to accept your love, but are so unwilling to demonstrate it. We are so eager to accept your mercy, but so unwilling to give it.

While we have known that Jesus did not come into the world to condemn it, we have believed that it is our responsibility to condemn it. While we have known that Jesus said he did not come into the world to judge it, we have believed it is our responsibility to judge it. While we have known that Jesus told his followers to "judge not," we have instead decided to judge anyway. And while we have known that Paul asked the Church, "What business is it of mine to judge those outside the Church?" we have instead decided that we should be the judges of the world? God forgive us for not being like Jesus to the world.

Father, we need the strength to sacrifice our own wants, needs, desires, and pursuits. Forgive us for the ways we have put idols within the Church ahead of you and your Kingdom. Forgive us for the way we have worshipped facility and program over you. Forgive us for the way we have followed human convention rather than your Spirit.

Father, we desperately need the fresh breath of your Holy Spirit to mold us and shape us into something useable and to open our eyes to the things that are not important to you. We know that while we have been ignorant and negligent in understanding and extending your Kingdom, our calling and pursuit should be to model Christ by living and extending your Kingdom, giving ourselves self-sacrificially in love and service to the world, embodying a life of peace, justice, and mercy that becomes the yearning of all humanity. Father, it is in this calling and pursuit that we have fallen woefully and painfully short. And it is because of our shortcomings with the world that we desperately need forgiveness.

Father, we need your power and strength to apologize to and seek forgiveness from any and all of those who have been on the receiving end of judgment, condemnation, or abuse from those of us who have labeled ourselves as Christians. We deeply and prayerfully apologize and repent. We have not represented the love, grace, mercy, and heart of Jesus very well…and we desperately need your forgiveness and the forgiveness of the world.

To the atheist, agnostic, Jew, and Muslim, we prayerfully ask for your forgiveness. To the homosexual, African-American, or any other minority that we have judged and oppressed in the past, we prayerfully ask for your forgiveness. To the poor, enslaved, or victim of injustice and abuse, we prayerfully ask for your forgiveness for judging you and turning a blind eye. And to every single person who has experienced anything less than the unconditional love of Christ from the Christian, we prayerfully ask for your forgiveness.

In Jesus name we as the Church in unity pray, Amen and Amen.

Notes

1. It will no longer be viewed as important to put priority on judging and evaluating every "church service" that we go to, in order to make sure that "we are getting appropriately fed." It will no longer be viewed as important to put priority on judging and evaluating how the preacher preached on Sunday or how the worship team performed. It will no longer be viewed as important to put priority on and be more concerned with what we can *get* at a "church service." Rather, as we turn and face outward, we will begin to prioritize what we can *give out* sacrificially to others?

2. State of Food Insecurity in the World, 2008 FAO."Food Security Statistics". www.fao.org/es/ess/faostat/foodsecurity/index_en.htm

3. This story is based upon the Old Testament indictment of the Israelites by God in Isaiah 1: 10-18.

4. The parable of the sheep and goats in Matthew 25: 31-46

5. Matthew 13: 24-30.

6. Matthew 23: 25-26.

7. Matthew 23: 27-28.

8. Isaiah 59: 9-10.

9. Katz, Arthur. The Mystery of Israel and the Church. Used by permission Art Katz Ministries.

10. Kinnaman, David. UnChristian: What a New Generation Thinks About Christianity...and Why it Matters. Ada: Baker Publishing Group, 2007.

11. Matthew 13: 1-23.

12. Ephesians 5:14.

13. This is a true story but I left out a portion of it because it was not relevant to my point. The guy actually was not very nice to me when I asked him to explain his perspective. He told me at the end of our conversation that "people like [you] will never get it." Well I did get it and I forgive you for being a jerk about it. How about that?

14. This original story is based upon Isaiah 5: 1-7.

15. This original story continues on the same idea about the vineyard from Isaiah 5 and continues the indictment from God. This time the indictment is directed to the Church.

16. Matthew 28: 18-20.

17. James 2: 20.
18. James 2: 19.
19. This original story is based upon Luke 11: 21-23.
20. Boyd, Greg. God at War. Chicago: InterVarsity Press, 1997.
21.
22. 1 John 5:19.
23. Ephesians 2:2.
24. 2 Corinthians 4:4.
25. Matthew 4: 1-11.
26. Leviticus 25: 8-55.
27. Luke 13: 18-19.
28. Luke 13: 20.
29. In his book *Jesus the Jewish Theologian* Brad Young contends that Matthew 11: 12 was rooted in the understanding of Micah 2: 12-13 and can be more accurately translated as, "From the days of John the Baptist until now, the Kingdom of [God] breaks forth and those breaking forth are pursuing [seeking] it." The imagery of the Kingdom breaking out like sheep in a sheep pen led by the King was rooted in the Micah 2 passage.
30. The best translation of Matthew 16: 18 is from The Message which describes the Church as an offensive movement that is, "so expansive with energy that not even the gates of hell will be able to keep it out." Gates are defensive structures not offensive weapons. The gates of hell will not stand because the Church is breaking down the strong holds.
31. Luke 4:43.
32. 2 Corinthians 5: 17.
33. Katz, Arthur. The Mystery of Israel and the Church. Used by permission Art Katz Ministries.
34. Hebrews 12: 25-29.
35. Luke 17: 20-21.
36. This passage was influenced by Revelation 12: 10-11.
37. John 15: 5-8.
38. Weirsbe, Warren. Real Worship. Nashville: Thomas Nelson Publishing, 1986.
39. Ephesians 6: 12.
40. 2 Corinthians 4: 10.
41. Colossians 3: 5-10.

42. Ephesians 6: 13-18.
43. 1 Corinthians 9: 25-27.
44. James 5: 16.
45. I really like using the imagery of coming out from behind the plants and shrubs standing naked before God because it draws us back to the account of Adam and Eve hiding *behind* the plants and shrubs from God because of their sin.
46. Matthew 6: 16.
47. Matthew 9: 15.
48. We believe in one God, the Father, the Almighty, maker of heaven and earth, of all that is, seen and unseen. We believe in one Lord, Jesus Christ, the only son of God, eternally begotten of the Father, God from God, Light from Light, true God from true God, begotten, not made, of one being with the Father. Through him all things were made. For us and for our salvation he came down from heaven: by the power of the Holy Spirit he became incarnate from the Virgin Mary, and was made man. For our sake he was crucified under Pontius Pilate; he suffered death and was buried. On the third day he rose again in accordance with the Scriptures; he ascended into heaven and is seated at the right hand of the Father. He will come again in glory to judge the living and the dead, and his kingdom will have no end. We believe in the Holy Spirit, the Lord, the giver of life, who proceeds from the Father [and the Son]. With the Father and the Son he is worshipped and glorified. He has spoken through the Prophets. We believe in one holy catholic and apostolic Church. We acknowledge one baptism for the forgiveness of sins. We look for the resurrection of the dead, and the life of the world to come. Amen.
49. Matthew 24: 14.
50. Acts 28: 30-31.
51. 1 Corinthians 1: 13-15.
52. This original story is based upon the parable of the talents in Matthew 25: 14-30.
53. Matthew 5: 13.
54. Matthew 5: 14.
55. Matthew 13: 24-30.
56. Matthew 9: 11-13.
57. Matthew 9: 37.

58. Isaiah 6: 8.
59. Matthew 10: 16.
60. Revelation 19: 6-8.
61. Matthew 6: 10.
62. Colossians 1: 15-20.
63. 1 Corinthians 15: 21-28.
64. Revelation 11: 15.
65. Sweet, Leonard, Viola, Frank. Jesus Manifesto. Nashville: Thomas Nelson Publishing, 2010.
66. Barna, George. Revolution. Carol Stream: Tyndale House (Barna Books), 2005.
67. Finney, Charles. Power From on High. Christian Literature Crusade, 1962.
68. 1 Corinthians 4: 12-13.
69. 1 Timothy 1: 15.
70. 1 Corinthians 12: 19-24.
71. Bonhoeffer, Dietrich. Life Together. Harper One, 1978.
72. 1 Peter 2: 9.

LaVergne, TN USA
29 October 2010
202678LV00004B/4/P